WHAT CHILDREN NEED WHEN THEY GRIEVE

The Four Essentials:
Routine, Love, Honesty, and Security

JULIA WILCOX RATHKEY

FOREWORD BY BARBARA BUSH
INTRODUCTION BY CYNTHIA R. PFEFFER, M.D.

THREE RIVERS PRESS • NEW YORK

Published by Three Rivers Press, New York, New York.
Member of the Crown Publishing Group, a division of Random House, Inc.
www.randomhouse.com

Three Rivers Press and the Tugboat design are registered trademarks of Random House, Inc.

Printed in the United States of America

Design by Meryl Sussman Levavi/Digitext

Library of Congress Cataloging-in-Publication Data
Rathkey, Julia Wilcox.
What children need when they grieve : the four essentials :
routine, love, honesty, and security / Julia Wilcox Rathkey ;
foreword by Barbara Bush ;
introduction by Cynthia R. Pfeffer.—1st ed.
p   cm.
1. Grief in children. 2. Bereavement in children.
3. Loss (Psychology) in children. 4. Child rearing. I. Title.
BF723.G75 R38 2004
155.9'37'083—dc22
2003019687

ISBN 1-4000-5116-9

10 9 8 7 6 5 4 3 2 1

First Edition

To David.
I always told you I'd get published.
Never did I imagine that it would be
because of losing you.

Acknowledgments

The strength and love my children and I have received since David's death have been inspirational and regenerative. Family, friends, and strangers alike have helped us to move forward and to live again with optimism and happiness in our hearts. Their love has given us the power to confront, again and again, some truly overwhelming thoughts and feelings as well as the courage to allow the world to see our vulnerabilities in hopes that others will find strength through our story. More specifically, I would like to thank my agent, Coleen O'Shea, for believing in my work and securing me a wonderful editor and publishing house with which to work. Becky Cabaza and the staff at Three Rivers Press have been a new author's dream. Becky remained patient and supportive throughout my writing process as I bumbled along as only a first-time writer can. Thank you, Coleen and Becky, for helping me produce a better book. Additionally, I am deeply indebted to former First Lady Barbara Bush for writing such a touching Foreword, and to Mrs. Bush's daughter, Doro, for putting me in touch with her mom. The introduction for my book, by Dr. Cynthia Pfeffer, is equally important, and I have enjoyed having the opportunity to get to know such a remarkable woman. I must also thank Amal Hussein for her honesty and willingness to critique my first draft. She told me what, in my heart, I knew I needed to do. Michael Grohman and Seresa El-Gafy both helped me in so many ways that I could never say thank you enough. So, too, must I thank Ray Best for all he has done. My sister, Elizabeth, has been my guide from the beginning of this process. A few months ahead of me in publishing her own first book, she has given me endless advice, support, and love. I would also like to thank my parents and other siblings for always being there. And lastly, I would like to thank my children. This book would not have been possible without their consent. The courage, love, and understanding they have shown have been beyond their years. Their willingness to expose themselves for the benefit of others is exemplary. No one could ask for more wonderful chidren, and I am filled with pride and love for them.

Contents

Foreword

Life changed for all Americans on September 11, 2001, as we realized our world would never be the same again. For most of us, it was the shock of how vulnerable we were to terrorism, the fear that it might happen again, and a feeling of a loss of innocence.

But for a much smaller group of Americans, the grief and shock they suffered on that horrible day were much more personal: Someone they knew and loved died, leaving behind a world that was more than changed; it was shattered.

Such was the case for Julia Wilcox Rathkey. Her husband, David, a sales executive at IQ Financial Systems, was killed in the World Trade Center, leaving her with their three young children to raise—a daughter, Emma, and twin boys, Matthew and Ian.

However, one of the first things Julia realized was that she really did not have the luxury to grieve her husband's death. Instead, she needed to cope with the broken hearts of her children. And with that difficult reality, Julia began a new journey in her life—one that is still continuing—and one which she has decided to share in this remarkable book, *What Children Need When They Grieve*.

I was hesitant at first to write this Foreword for the simple reason I had never met Julia. But when I started paging through her book, I felt like I had. And I immediately liked and admired her. In my seventy-eight years, I have watched many people struggle with the loss of a loved one, and I've always been in awe of those people who find the strength and courage to turn their tragedy into a force for good. That is exactly what Julia did by taking the time to document her journey of grief and recovery with her children. It is a wonderful gift for those parents who, unfortunately, might one day face the same challenges she has every single day since September 11. Thanks to Julia, hopefully they will find not only some helpful advice in these pages, but some comfort in knowing that they are not alone.

BARBARA BUSH

Introduction

I am honored to be invited to write the Introduction to this important book, *What Children Need When They Grieve*. A very courageous mother wrote it. Her beloved husband, David, died as a result of the tragic terrorist attacks on September 11, 2001, while he was at work in the World Trade Center in New York City. One of Julia Wilcox Rathkey's important aims in writing this book was to share her experiences with other parents and caretakers of children who lost their parents as a result of this horrific event. She hoped it would provide guidance to the large number of parents and caretakers of children and adolescents who suffered losses of relatives on this tragic day as well as those who lost a loved one from other causes. Her aim was to help bereaved parents or caretakers assist their grieving children in coping with their monumental loss. Firsthand accounts of the experiences of those afflicted by a severe, stressful event, such as the sudden, unexpected death of a loved one, offer essential qualitative information that can be helpful not only to grieving families but also to others, such as professionals and friends who assist such families. Such accounts also offer guideposts for those planning systematic studies to understand the developmental patterns of children who have suffered grief.

This book is written in a direct, sensitive manner by a mother who is so devoted to her children that she put aside many of her overwhelming feelings of grief in order to focus on the needs of her children during their bereavement resulting from the death of their father. As an author of this book, she is a fine teacher. She illustrates her ideas with clear examples. Her topics are relevant and define specific needs that children have when they are suffering the bereavement of a loved one. The images of her perceptions are profoundly moving and provide persuasive evidence of the feelings, behaviors, and wishes of her children as they attempt to cope with their significant loss. She presents her ideas with great humility. She recognizes that her concepts may not be generalized to all grieving children. This enables her concepts to be considered, reflected upon, and even questioned. Her style of openness is a model to point out to other parents or caretakers of grieving children that there are distinct ways of communicating with children about their loss. Her message is that children's grief may take varied forms. This complicates parents' abilities to offer solace in many of the daily life circumstances affected by the process of children's bereavement.

Mrs. Rathkey points out that children have intense grief responses that vary over time. Such responses are not similar for all children. Boys may express their grief differently from girls. Young children's grief may appear to be different from that of teenagers. Many other developmental issues are important to understand and respond to, often in unique ways.

While Mrs. Rathkey's personal experience involves her three children, Emma, twelve years old, and her twin sons, Ian and Matthew, ten years old, when their father died, empirical information suggests that developmental issues strongly influence the manifestations of children's grieving processes. Four important patterns influence children's bereavement characteristics. Children's immaturity affects their concepts of death and capacity for coping with loss. Children have limited capacities to tolerate intense emotional pain. Children have limited abilities to verbalize their feelings. And children are very sensitive about being different from their peers. Therefore, as this mother described, it is essential to listen, support, encourage, and guide children when they express their bereavement concerns. In addition, as noted by this mother, parents need to respect the developmental differences of their children's expressions of grief.

Grief is a very stressful experience that is an expected response to the loss of loved ones. Patterns of children's grief indicate that as cognitive functions mature, the grief responses appear more like those of adults. However, this does not manifest until middle to late adolescence. At this time, grieving adolescents seek support not only from parents but also from peers. They understand the finality and processes leading to death. They may be resentful and angry as well as sad and may avoid certain school and social activities. They may be extensively preoccupied with memories of the deceased and the meanings the deceased had in their daily lives as role models and guides. They may feel guilty about an interaction or lack of involvement with the deceased.

In contrast, infants respond to loss with physical reactions, including problems eating and sleeping and excessive crying. When children are in their second and third years, they begin to comprehend that death involves a separation. This is associated with anxiety and feelings of insecurity upon separation from caretaking adults. They may exhibit thumb sucking, which serves to soothe. They may cling to caretakers. As children get older, they may think they have magical powers to bring back the deceased. Their concepts of the permanence of death are not developed yet.

Schoolchildren, who are age six years and older, ask many questions about the deceased and the cause of death. They express concerns about missing the deceased. They may carry on conversations with the deceased. Some may say they, too, want to die to be with the deceased. This preoccupation requires close monitoring and if it persists, consultation with a mental health professional is suggested. Children of this developmental level may develop repeated behaviors as a means of remembering the deceased. They may pray at bedtime or have repeated behaviors as means of maintaining a close feeling with the deceased. Often, school-children have persistent fears about the safety and health of their living parent. However, they may also show anger and irritability and defy limits set up by the surviving parent. For children, the surviving parent cannot make up entirely for the profound loss of a parent. Schoolchildren may not be entirely open in expressing their feelings. They may withdraw from discussions about the deceased. They may prefer to be alone and think about their loss. They may appear as if they do not care that their parent has died.

The significance of this personal account of Mrs. Rathkey's perceptions of her children's grief cannot be underestimated. It also represents the process of her grief that is complicated by her parental role and tasks as caretaker. At present, there is relatively little systematic information on the course of children's bereavement. Yet children's experiences with the loss of loved ones through death are relatively common, especially as a result of wars, accidents, illnesses, and natural disasters. This book is especially pertinent since thousands of children suffered the sudden, unexpected, homicidal death of a parent on September 11, 2001. This was a unique event. It certainly sensitized the world to the significance of bereavement. It certainly stimulated extensive and varied community efforts to assist such children and their families. It pointed out the essentialness of acquiring extensive and systematic information about how children cope with the death of a loved one. This book offers clues to guide this important mission.

The book points out that grieving is an essential aspect

of children's coping with the permanent disappearance of a parent. As is scientifically suggested, this book highlights that permanent loss resulting from the death of a child's parents stimulates nascent responses that are part of human emotions. Such grief emotions are called into play as a means of fostering children's adaptations to the irreparable change in their lives. Gradually, the knowledge of how the death occurred is incorporated with the realization of the preeminence of the loss. Such processes take time. Positive adaptation can occur through efforts of others lending consistent support in the form of encouragement, optimism, and teaching of skills for coping with daily life events. Mrs. Rathkey says it best with her model of offering to children routine, love, honesty, and security.

This is a book that should be read by all parents, regardless of whether their children suffered the loss of a loved one. It is essential for professionals, including psychiatrists, psychologists, social workers, school professionals, pediatricians, clergy, and others who may be in the role of interacting with children and their families. I believe that this book will enable many families to garner renewed strength, plan for positive futures, and realize that unexpected losses may present challenges that may promote positive outcomes for children.

CYNTHIA R. PFEFFER, M.D.

PROFESSOR OF PSYCHIATRY;

DIRECTOR OF THE CHILDHOOD BEREAVEMENT PROGRAM,

WEILL MEDICAL COLLEGE OF CORNELL UNIVERSITY,

WHITE PLAINS, NEW YORK

PART ONE

CONFRONTING LOSS

Our Story

On September 11, 2001, my husband, David, was killed by terrorists in the attack on the World Trade Center. We had just celebrated our fifteenth wedding anniversary. We had met each other over the Atlantic on a flight from London to New York. He was English and I am American. It was a match made in heaven, or certainly pretty close to it given our altitude at the time. We had three beautiful, happy children to show from our years together. Emma was twelve, and identical twins, Ian and Matthew, were ten. We had a fun family vacation planned for November when we were going to celebrate our anniversary and my upcoming fortieth birthday. Never did we anticipate the turn of events on that terrible day.

It started out as a very normal day. No different from

any other. David got up and got ready for work while we all still slept peacefully in our beds. He didn't go in to say good-bye to the children because he didn't like to wake them, so that morning the children never got to kiss him. He always woke me up, though, and I still remember his kiss good-bye that soon-to-be-dreadful morning.

School had just started for the children the previous week, and all three were enjoying being back with their friends and adjusting to their new schedules and teachers. It was fun until that day.

I was at home when I heard the news, just on my way out the door. My brother called to tell me that a plane had hit the World Trade Center. I immediately tried calling David but got no reply on his work or cell phone. After that, I ran upstairs to turn on the television to see what exactly was going on. As soon as I saw the screen, my heart leapt and I felt dizzy. A gaping hole was in the same building David worked in, and right around the area of David's office.

Not knowing what to do, I called two friends who came over immediately. Frantically, I tried every way I knew how to get in touch with David. Then, miraculously, he called. I thought he was safe. I started talking away, asking questions, but he quickly interrupted me and told me that he was trapped on the eighty-third floor. He was surrounded by smoke and was with two female colleagues, whom he was trying to comfort and protect. They had no way of escape. David had been just below the point of impact when the plane struck the building because he had been in a meeting on a floor beneath his office. After the plane hit, people around him were discussing the need to evacuate when an announcement was made over the loudspeaker. Workers were told to return to their offices, and that there was no need to evacuate. David took the elevator up to his office on the eighty-third floor and waited for further instruction. Shortly thereafter, everyone realized the necessity of getting out of the building. Waiting patiently for an elevator to arrive, there was limited space with the mass exodus and David graciously stood back, saying that he would wait for another elevator to arrive. One never did.

With this final phone call, David wanted the children and me to know that he loved us very much. He was trying to get out and had called 911, but the smoke was thick and his chest was tight and burning. He had plenty of water, though, and a handkerchief with which to cover his mouth. I promised him that I would try to get help and I instructed him on what to do in a smoke-filled room. I even made suggestions on how he could perhaps get to the stairs, using desks or chairs as a guiding path. After too brief a conversation, David said that he had to go because it was becoming difficult to talk. He was struggling to find air. Reluctantly, I hung up the phone.

Immediately, I was overwhelmed with a feeling of panic and helplessness. What could I do to help David? I had to be there for him. How could I save him? I frantically called 911, the New York City Police Department, our local police department, and anyone else I could think of who might be able to help. Everywhere was in chaos, and as time marched on and I was getting no closer to saving David, I knew time was running out. As my swell of fear and panic rose, I watched the towers fall.

Immediately, my first thought was for my children. I quickly called their two schools. I needed to know if the schools had said anything to the students, and if so, what. Additionally, if nothing had been announced, were they planning on telling the students anything at all? Both Emma's middle school and Ian and Matthew's elementary school assured me that nothing had been announced to the children, and that nothing would be said during the course of the day. The schools intended to shield the students until dismissal, at which point it was up to the parents to determine what would be said.

Confident my children were oblivious to the unfolding disaster, I took a deep breath. I needed time to clear my head, collect my composure as best as I could, and to think. I didn't know for sure that David was dead so I had to handle the situation as well as I was able when I picked up my kids from school. I needed to get some answers.

Sometime after my phone conversation with Emma's middle school, the strategy of the school changed. Amid all the chaos, unbeknownst to me, an announcement was made informing the students that a plane had hit the World Trade Center. Nothing was mentioned of the collapse. The children were then told that anyone who was worried about a family member could go into the office and try to reach his or her parents. Knowing that her dad worked there, Emma went to the office immediately. She tried calling home several times but the phone was busy and she couldn't get through. A friend of the family who'd been at the school that morning had seen Emma and came rushing over to my house to let me know that Emma was very worried and upset. As soon as I found out that Emma had learned something of the disaster, I quickly jumped in my friend's car and rushed to her school.

My friend arrived with the news of Emma's distress so shortly after the collapse of the towers that I hadn't had much time to think things through, and my head was still swimming. I was extremely frightened about telling the children because I knew how painful it would be for them. I also knew that I didn't really have any answers, or at least none that would be comforting.

Nervously, I rushed into the middle school office. Knowing why I was there, the administrator told me that Emma was waiting in the guidance counselor's office. Emma must have somehow heard my voice because we both emerged in the hallway at the same time. Emma was clearly distraught and crying hard. Her body was shaking. She looked at me with pleading, wishful eyes, and when I frowned and slightly shook my head, we collapsed into each other's arms, melting into each other, wanting to disappear. We stood motionless. The only movement was our shaking shoulders; the only sound was our sobs. Slowly, we crept out of the building, off to tell Emma's twin brothers at their elementary school.

At Ian and Matthew's school, the children knew nothing of the disaster. The office paged the boys and asked them to come upstairs. I'll never forget their innocent, smiling faces as, one at a time, they appeared in the hallway. Ian was the first to emerge, happy to see us but curious as to why Emma and I were at school. He thought that I was picking them up early because Emma had a doctor's appointment. From his distance, he couldn't see our red, tear-swollen eyes. As he neared, I reached out and hugged him tightly. He now knew something was wrong, but I didn't want to tell him until Matthew came up. I escorted him into a quiet, private office and told him to wait until Matthew arrived. I'm sure he was terrified. There was a counselor with him and Ian became increasingly more concerned about what was going on. Once I found Matthew, I took him in to join his brother. I had wanted to sweep them away and tell them what was going on once we got home, but somehow events overtook me and the counselor started speaking about the tragedy. My children were both confused and distraught. We all sat there numb, crying, and upset. Not sure what to do, I picked up their belongings and we were silently driven home. The car ride was a surreal experience of touch, tears, and disbelief. Consumed with shock, we didn't speak until we entered our house, when I tried to explain what was going on with their father and the World Trade Center's collapse. It was nearly impossible for us to explain or comprehend anything.

Months later, the boys told me that when I told them the World Trade Center had been hit by a plane and collapsed, they weren't sure quite what was going on. They said that they didn't know that Dad's office building was the World Trade Center. Ian had always referred to David's office as being in the Twin Towers. Matthew didn't even realize that his father worked in the Twin Towers. The connection between the Twin Towers and the World Trade Center didn't occur in their young minds. Emma's and my fear was what initially had terrified them so much. They knew that something terrible had happened to their father but they couldn't quite piece it together. It wasn't until later in our discussion that they realized the full implication of what I was telling them.

With that first conversation I had already made a mistake. I had made assumptions for my children that I shouldn't have. It was important for me to realize that I would be dealing with a very different understanding and perspective from my own. I needed to communicate better with my children. I needed to make sure that they understood what I was saying and doing.

Thus, after the initial shock of the collapse of the buildings and David's presumed death, my first fear was for my children. How would I help them through this? What could I possibly do to make this less difficult for them? How could they digest all the uncertainty and intangibility of the situation and apply it to losing their father?

I felt immediately that David had not survived the disaster. That evening, I was aware of a very strong presence around me that I knew to be David comforting me. He was gone. Now I needed to help the children, and to give them the strength that David was giving me. So, in the wake of uncertainty and death, I attempted to help console my children with books. I consumed book after book, looking for the answer, hoping to find the perfect guidance and explanation for this bizarre and frightening tragedy. I had friends go on searches for books about grief and loss that I could share with my children. Each time we failed. Somehow, nothing seemed to be right. I resented reading books from people who had never experienced grief. How could they possibly know how I felt? Experience is the only true frame of reference with grief. It made me angry when they professed to know the answers when they didn't even have the questions. I needed personalization. I needed to identify with someone else's grief.

My children felt this way, too. Nothing we read seemed to fit how we felt. It wasn't the tragedy we needed to identify with, because there was no tragedy comparable to ours. It was someone else's own thoughts and feelings that we needed, someone else's numbness and fear, but also someone else's struggle for normalcy and strength. We needed to know that we were not alone, and that others were able to understand and feel our pain. But we also needed guidance. We needed to gain strength.

This book is about parenting and guiding children through the grieving process. It is designed to help a child come to terms with grief and to gain strength through grief. It is directed toward any caregiver, and by *caregiver* I mean a mother or father or any adult who has the primary responsibility for a child. In most instances this probably will be a parent or guardian, but if you are reading this and happen to be a teacher, a mental health professional, a babysitter, or any relative or adult friend of a grieving child or family, then I hope you find this book to be of help.

The death of my husband, David, was a very public tragedy. The kindness and support my children and I received from family, friends, our community, and complete strangers was inspirational and overwhelming. It gave us a great deal of additional strength. On the flip side, we sometimes found it hard to catch a moment of privacy and anonymity. Everywhere I went, people saw my face or heard my name and immediately knew my private agony. Comments and discussions about the World Trade Center were on every media station and in every supermarket aisle. It was hard to protect the children from statements that might upset them. When my daughter didn't eat her school lunch, I would receive phone calls and questions asking me whether Emma was developing an eating disorder. I recognize that people were only trying to help or to come to terms with the tragedy themselves, but sometimes I just wanted to disappear. I also wanted to cover my children with a protective bubble.

Regardless of your situation, and regardless of the support you may or may not receive, helping a grieving child is never easy. All caregivers must endure different hardships, and all paths will be different. My path was easier than most, because of the extraordinary support my children and I received, and for that I am truly grateful. But we are all united in our ultimate goal of helping a grieving child to heal. In my experience, I learned that the journey toward healing encompasses what I call the four essentials—routine, love, honesty, and security—and each of these things manifests itself in very practical ways. Armed with this knowledge, any adult in any situation can successfully battle a child's demons of grief. In this book, using clear examples, I'd like to share with you some of my positive discoveries and negative pitfalls of what my children and I had to endure during our ongoing journey. My combined philosophy of routine, love, and honesty gave my children the security needed to rise above their sadness. No one essential was independent of the other. All four essentials were needed at all times to guide my children.

What Children Need When They Grieve is for any adult who has to struggle with any type of grieving child, not only a child who has lost a parent. You, as a parent or caregiver, may be facing the death of your spouse or partner, a sibling, parent, or grandparent or other relative, a close friend or perhaps a child. While you may undoubtedly be shouldering the huge burden of your own grief, you are reading this book because this person was also a major and beloved figure in your child's life. Even if you do not have to battle your own grief, or perhaps the loss is someone unrelated to your child's family, such as a classmate, the road for you will still be challenging, your child's grief may still be consuming. For any of these scenarios, this book will be your road map.

I am neither a professional nor a counselor. I have no qualifications other than my experience as a mother and a widow. I have my grief and my children's grief as my guide. I have my experience as a mother and my love for my children and husband as my strength.

I want to develop my children into happy, loving, and responsible individuals who are not afraid to laugh and to cry, individuals who can openly remember their father without pain but with fondness, joy, and love. I want to help them through their grief and enable them to become stronger, more compassionate people.

Grief is a terrible emotion to endure. But it is a part of life. Eventually we will all confront it, even if it is our own death we grieve. Children, with their limited life experience and immaturity, especially need help with this process. I hope this book will help you to help the children in your life.

PART TWO

REACTIONS TO LOSS

Grief and Fear

Grief

FOR CHILDREN, LIFE IS INNOCENT AND SECURE. When they lose a loved one, they go from a world of trust and protection to one of uncertainty and fear. They cannot understand how such a loss could have happened. They suddenly have a new perspective on life, and struggle to comprehend death. Adults, too, struggle with these feelings and ideas, but children lose some of their innocence and security.

The day that my husband, David, died, my children were thrust into a whirlwind of insecurities and fear. Death was no longer an intangible, a far-removed form of entertainment in their cartoons, but a gut-wrenching reality.

I vividly remember my son Matthew's first action when he entered the house after hearing what had happened to his father. He ran upstairs to his bedroom, grabbed a picture of his dad, and gently placed it on his bed. He then spent the next couple of minutes trying to take in through his swollen, teary eyes every detail of David. It was as if he wanted to never forget any part of his father, and he wanted to hold on to those memories and cherish them. He was trying to reach out to his dad and to be able to touch him for one last time. He wanted to be alone with his memories and pain, trying to comprehend the enormity of what had just transpired in his young life.

That image of Matthew's suffering still torments me. I could do nothing to change his reality and to remove the agony of his grief.

As a parent, your mission is to raise as healthy and happy a child as you are able. You hope that your children will be free from as much stress and hardship as you can possibly control. You take great effort to throw them a birthday party or to plan a vacation that will bring pure joy and delight to their beaming faces; and you try to protect and heal them when they are hurt or afraid. But when your children are grieving, you are no longer in control and you can no longer always get them to smile or feel secure. You feel their pain, and it breaks your heart to see them suffer. In addition, you may be suffering your own grief from the loss of the loved one. In that way, you must endure a kind of double grief. You grieve for the loved one and you grieve for your children.

How Children Experience Grief

The grieving process is very different for every person who experiences it. We each bring with us different family dynamics and life experiences, in addition to our own unique relationship with the loved one we are grieving for. All three of my children reacted differently to the loss of their father. My daughter, who is very quiet and self-controlled, didn't display much emotion other than sudden, infrequent outbursts of sorrow. She didn't really want to talk about her feelings, but she would sometimes listen. My son Ian was very emotional. He cried openly and needed me to reassure him. He also displayed a lot of anger. Matthew was in total denial. Every time I mentioned David, or anyone wanted to talk to him about how he was feeling, he would say he was fine and walk away.

So just as every person is different, so is his or her grief. There is no formula as to how an individual should or shouldn't react. One person might want and need to spend hours with a therapist, while another might want to be completely alone with his or her thoughts or surround oneself with family. One person might yell and scream all day, whereas another might smile and stay calm. There is no way to predict what someone might do at any given moment. They don't even know themselves. Minute to minute, day to day, emotions and thoughts change. A certain smell, sight, or sound can unleash a torrent of tears when one minute ago they felt perfectly calm and in control. Grief is unpredictable.

I decided that my children should attend some therapy sessions. (I attended therapy myself, and I'll describe this further in the next chapter.) My philosophy was that it wouldn't hurt them and perhaps it might help. At the time, I didn't feel like I was making much progress with handling their grief, so I felt that maybe an objective professional would have better luck. Looking back, I realize that I was too impatient with grief. One must allow time for seemingly little progress. Grief has its own timetable for each person.

In all honesty, it was Matthew who was the impetus for their therapy sessions. I did have all three children talking with their school guidance counselors, but I hadn't yet looked for someone more specialized in dealing with grief. One day, Matthew actually told his school counselor that he needed to speak with someone else. He needed another professional, and he needed more help. Quickly, I started researching for a mental health professional who specialized in children's grief. The professional I was seeing was very good, but the drive was too far for me to continue going there for either my children or myself. I knew it would be difficult for me to find a professional equipped to handle a death such as David's as this was new territory for everyone. Additionally, there weren't a lot of coordinated resources available before 9/11. Fortunately or unfortunately, since that date, many resources have emerged or have become more organized. (See "Professional Sources of Guidance" at the end of this book for some suggestions.) Still, I went the normal route of asking my pediatrician, my existing grief counselor, and various friends. Finally, I called my local hospital and inquired about their mental health facility. Seeing as my insurance covered the hospital's program and I was able to make an immediate appointment, I brought my children there.

Neither of my other two children wanted to go to therapy, especially my daughter. They yelled and screamed when I told them that they would have to try it, and all their protests affected Matthew's attitude. Suddenly, he was revoking his previous cry for help. It was emotionally exhausting for me to battle with them. "It's not going to hurt you," I'd say. "Maybe it will help."

I made sure that each child had a separate appointment. I didn't want one to feel embarrassed about what they said or did in front of their siblings. In defiance, Ian sat staring out the window with his back to the therapist the entire session. He felt very spiteful toward me and proudly told me what he had done and that he never even said a word. My daughter said all the right things, trying to outsmart the therapist. Matthew, despite his earlier protest, seemed relatively content, although, feeling sibling pressure, he caved in and began complaining.

Afterward, after hearing their complaints, I told them that if they hated it so much I would compromise, but that they had to be willing to compromise, too. I told them that they would have to do therapy at least once a week for one month. Then we could reassess. However, if my children refused to participate in any form of dialogue with their counselor, they would have to carry on with more sessions. If they really were having difficulty, I would find them a new therapist. I felt very strongly that they had to give the therapy a chance. I wasn't sure which way to turn with their grief and I felt that I needed to explore every angle. Also, I had to remember that Matthew had reached out and actually *asked* for help. This was very contrary to his behavior since David's death as it was the first time he had actually opened up and addressed his grief. I needed to respond to that cry for help. If Emma and Ian refused therapy, I doubted that Matthew would have the strength to go through it alone. Sometimes, siblings may have to make sacrifices in order to help each other. Grief involves reaching out.

As it turned out, the therapist released Emma after about two months. Emma believed she had successfully accomplished her goal of outsmarting her. Actually, I felt she was at a place where she needed her friends and my support more than advice from a stranger, regardless of how professional. Also, my worries about understanding what Emma needed had been confirmed by her counselor, and as a result, I felt much more confident with my parenting.

The boys continued with their therapy until the spring, when again, I felt it had served its purpose for the time being. All three of them didn't mind the counseling as much once they understood what it was all about. They adjusted to it. The boys didn't even complain too much when Emma was released and they still had to carry on. None of them really enjoyed going, though, and I still had the occasional, brief battle.

Therapy can be emotionally painful, and it would have been easier for my children to stay home and play on the computer or watch television. But I stayed strong, making them attend, and, as their mother, knowing that this was in their best interest. Also, it was helpful to have another adult's unbiased perspective. I did find out some more things about my children's feelings, but I mostly learned what I already thought I knew: that I understood my children and that, more than anyone else, I had a clear picture of where they were in the grieving process. I learned to trust my instincts even more.

I realize that one day, one or all of them may need to return to therapy. Some people need it more than others and some may not need it at all. In my experience, it doesn't hurt, though, and it may ultimately be very beneficial, especially when the quality of the therapy is high.

Grief can cause indescribable pain. The permanent loss of a loved one, the thought that you will never see or talk with the deceased again, the change in life as you know it, is an overwhelming reality. The definition of *normal* has suddenly changed, and you are thrust into a very new and different life. This death was not your choice and it becomes very difficult to proceed with your new reality. You feel numb and can go through the motions only in order to survive. Sometimes even the motions of survival are too difficult. Focus is nearly impossible. Everything is a blur and time seems to stand still and accelerate at the same time.

But when an adult is responsible for the well-being of a child, grief is even more difficult. Because when a child is grieving, that child needs a caregiver to be his or her support. The child needs someone to hold his or her hand and to help him or her to survive. Grief of a caregiver cannot be selfish because the child must often come first. A child's grief can be just as debilitating to the child's existence as an adult's grief is to an adult's. A child's denial can be even more intense, because of his or her innocence.

There are stages of grief, but those, too, are not consistent or necessarily felt in any specific order. Shock, denial, guilt, and anger are all common feelings when a person is grieving. Typically, shock is the first reaction. It can last months or minutes, and can be accompanied by other feelings of grief for all or just part of the time. Denial, guilt, and anger can come and go. They can last varying amounts of time, and come in any order or even not at all. While one child is plagued with endless guilt, another might experience lasting anger. You might find that if your child didn't have time to say good-bye to a loved one, as my children didn't, that child may feel an overwhelming sense of guilt. This can be very difficult for them to work through.

In a similar vein, if a child's last conversation with a loved one was hostile, the guilt can be just as intense. Even if the child said good-bye or had a loving final conversation or memory, the child may be feeling guilty because the child is so angry with the deceased for the abandonment. In that instance, anger and guilt work hand in hand.

I know that Emma felt guilty about not saying good-bye to her father that fateful morning. She had been awake and had heard him getting ready for work. She lay in bed listening to him quietly walk around. He thought she was still asleep and didn't want to wake her. She didn't think to yell out to him because she never had before. And so without saying good-bye, she heard him slowly drive away.

Matthew felt guilty, too, but for a different reason. He finally confided in me that he had ignored his dad and been a bit short-tempered with him when David came in to say good night on their last evening together. It was because Matthew had been tired and in a bad mood. But now, Matthew was tormenting himself with guilt. He had been holding in his emotions for so long because he couldn't bear to even think about it. His last moments with his father had been hostile, and he wanted so much to reverse those moments and make them loving and positive. He cried so hard when he finally told me. He had been feeling so guilty.

We had the memorial service eleven days after David's death. One advantage to not having his body was that I had no time constraints for planning his memorial service. Perhaps unlike you or someone you know, I had the luxury of time in this instance.

So for David's memorial service, I wanted to give my children and myself some time to properly prepare for the service, and David's family had to make arrangements and fly over from England. For my children's sake, I also didn't want the memorial service to be delayed too long into the future and to drag out the anticipation of the event for them. My immediate planning of the service did cause quite a bit of friction between my husband's family and me. David's family would have preferred more time to come to terms with

David's sudden disappearance and to organize things a bit more before flying over to America. For a short while, I wasn't sure if they would come. However, as I continued to impress upon them that this was in the best interests of the children, my in-laws recognized my rationale and made arrangements.

Part of my rationale for having the service when I did was because I wanted to keep Emma, Ian, and Matthew home from school only until the time of the service. I felt that my kids needed to have that part behind them so that they could get back to school with some sort of closure.

I asked my children to help me with the service. I thought it would help them with their grief. I requested that my twelve-year-old daughter make the cover page of the memorial booklet with family pictures that I found. I also asked her if she would think about writing something to her father, which could be read by her uncle if she wasn't up to reading it herself. I couldn't imagine she would want to read it herself. I told her that I would also be writing but not reading something and that I was going to make the same suggestion to her twin brothers.

In the end, her ten-year-old brothers each drew a picture of a heart with their names and "Dad" written in each. One of my sons wrote additional thoughts on his picture, but neither wanted his drawings to be shared at the memorial service. My daughter did write a very moving letter, and created a beautiful cover page for the memorial service program with wonderful pictures surrounded by red hearts and blue snowflakes. In her letter Emma said how much she identified with her father and how much she enjoyed his companionship and guidance. She let everyone know how much she loved him. She wrote about their last evening together and what they did. She also wrote about the last morning her father was alive.

Here is her letter:

I have been sitting on my friend's bed for quite some time thinking of what to write for Saturday. I think of all the great things we did together and how I got along better with him than with my mom. I guess that's because people say I'm like my father. When you're like someone it seems as though you get along better with him or her much easier. Maybe it's just because my mom can't practice softball or soccer with me, or lie in front of the television watching hardware shows that I've always had some sort of interest in for some strange reason. I think of how he would always practice softball with me and he'd always wear one of my brother's gloves that was five sizes too small, and half of his hand would show, and how I've never been any good at throwing the ball so my dad would always have to leap to reach it, but my throw would be so bad that he would have to walk halfway across the yard to go and retrieve it. With his bad back, he would groan and hardly be able to pick up the ball, so with all my terrible throws his back would be killing him after a fifteen-minute game of catch. But it was funny because he would get mad at me for my bad sense of aim and I'd laugh and usually he'd give me a bad throw back and I'd have to walk in the weeds and bushes to go and get my softball. I never meant to miss his glove but I was born with this bad sense of aim and even if I tried to hit his glove, it would keep missing repeatedly.

Eventually, he'd get tired and we'd have to go in even though I really didn't want to. He made excuses like it's getting dark and he couldn't see the ball, or something like I had to take a shower and do my homework. Most of the time it was getting dark and I did have to do my homework, but I didn't care. I could get smacked in the head for all I cared (once I was too).

My father was also my soccer coach. He loved the sport and was overjoyed to teach my classmates and me. Even if some practices didn't go too well, or we were the worst in our division, he just had fun doing it. The last practice my dad was alive for I had been sick so I didn't play. I sat and I watched. I remember him coming over and asking me what I was working on and I said math and then he left and went back to teach the girls who had just come back from their jog around the field a couple of times. Then it started to thunder, and sure enough there was lightning and then it started to pour. Well my dad came back into the car and made sure everyone had a ride home, and when everyone did, we went home. That was the last night my father was alive. I remember the next morning, hearing him get up and thinking nothing of it, but now I wish I had said good-bye.

The last couple weeks of my father's life, he painted my room and we went on day trips to miniature golf and amusement parks and other places that I didn't really want to go. But in the end, I had fun and so did my dad. My father always wanted to go on bike rides and I said no way are you getting me on my bike. Well for some annoying reason, he always did and I was always stuck riding my bike all through town. I hated it but my father always made me do it cause I wasn't fit enough or something like that.

My cat was lost for two days and my father said she'd be fine and no need to worry. He went out looking for her with me and we didn't find her and still he said she'd be okay. Well, guess what? She was. She ended up just dandy. She came home and everything was just grand. Now I am sitting here at my computer and thinking of all the great things I did with my father and I realize that all I had to say were four words: *I loved my father.*

I think it helped my children to participate in the memorial service, even if it was a private contribution. It took them a long time to do what I had asked of them. Had they chosen not to do anything, that was fine with me, but I wanted to give them the opportunity; so I didn't pester them about it continually. I would occasionally remind them that I was hoping that they would do something before the service. I knew how hard it was for me to write something and it took a lot of courage and strength. It was a long time until I could put pen to paper. So, as days passed and my children produced nothing, I didn't worry. If they could, they would, when they were ready.

However, by eventually contributing to their father's memorial service, my children helped themselves to face their grief and confront their feelings in a way that they might not have had I not asked them. It was very hard and it was painful, but it helped us. It took away a little bit of the denial. It helped us in our grieving process.

I read to my children about grief, too. Given Emma's personality, she had no interest in listening to me. But somewhat reluctantly, the boys would sit on either side of me, entwined in my arms, and listen. I would cry as I attempted to get through the book. Sometimes I would have to compose myself before I could continue. They would often begin to cry along with me, and when I was done, we would just hold on to one another. I hated reading to them because it was so painful, but it would help us to cry with one another and to share in our loss.

Sometimes the grieving process lasts days or weeks, while other times it may last years. We are all still grieving, but we are healing, too. Don't try to put a time frame on anyone's grief. It is something each individual must work through and endure alone, although certain things can help the child get through the process with less pain.

What You Can Do to Help Your Child Confront Grief

- Recognize that each child will respond differently to grief.
- Don't compare reactions to loss and judge one child's reaction to be more "normal" than another's.
- A child cannot heal without your help. When children are involved, grief cannot be selfish. Though you

should take care of yourself, focus on your child's needs.

- Encourage your child to attend grief therapy. It will help you to better understand your child's reactions to loss.

- Shock, denial, guilt, and fear are all normal reactions during the grieving process. Talk with your child about these reactions to loss and help each child to understand the normalcy of these feelings.

- Try to get your child involved with the funeral/memorial service, either privately or more publicly. Depending on his or her age, ask your child to draw a picture, write a letter, or design some aspect of the service.

- Don't become impatient with the grieving process and expect your child (or yourself) to adjust to a loss within a specific time frame. Grief has its own timetable.

- Don't hide any pictures of the loved one. Instead, encourage your child to have the loved one's photo displayed in his or her room.

- Read to your child about loss. It will help to clarify things.

- Stay strong.

Fear

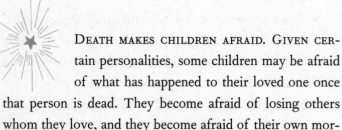 DEATH MAKES CHILDREN AFRAID. GIVEN CER-
tain personalities, some children may be afraid
of what has happened to their loved one once
that person is dead. They become afraid of losing others
whom they love, and they become afraid of their own mor-
tality. However, aside from the irresolvable fear of the certainty of death and its afterlife, there are other more tangible
fears in children that may be revealed to a caregiver and
slightly easier to address.

Depending on a child's age, personality, or environment, a child's reaction to death may elicit fear in many different ways or in a combination of ways. Sometimes
children may tell you exactly what they fear. Sometimes they
may just start acting out. You may have a child who becomes

panicky or unusually quiet. Be aware that every child experiences fear with the death of a loved one, and that it may manifest itself in many different ways.

I was afraid, too. One of my biggest fears was not knowing how to handle my children during this difficult time of grief. There is no guidebook for grief. I felt that I needed some guidance to help me and to make sure I was doing the right things. Within a few days after David's death, two friends of mine approached me about consulting a grief counselor whom they knew. They said that she was very good and could help me with my worries regarding my children. Immediately, I agreed, recognizing I had nothing to lose.

My only hesitation was that she lived quite far away and I wasn't sure that I would have the focus to drive. Also, I knew the meeting would be emotional and I was worried that I might be too much of a wreck to drive home. Without hesitation my friends made arrangements for me to be driven and for someone to watch the children.

Counseling is very difficult and easier to avoid. Emotional pain is draining, but I knew it was what needed to be done in order for me to heal and to help my children. It takes a lot of courage for anyone to put oneself through therapy but the rewards can be worth it. I recognized the benefits and forced myself to return to therapy until I felt I had what I needed to help my children and myself.

I attended about half a dozen sessions until I felt I had the necessary tools to cope with my children unguided. Rather than spend two to three hours traveling and attending a session, I decided that time was better spent being with my children. I had more confidence now. I knew I could always return or attend other therapy closer to home, but for the time being I wanted to be with my children. We needed to regroup as a family.

I am extremely glad I had the counseling. I desperately needed it to focus on my concerns regarding my kids. It helped me to clarify a lot of things I was worried about. It made me take a deep breath, prioritize, and give more thought to things that needed to be addressed more carefully. Given my highly emotional state, it was so easy for me to panic and to rush into a bad or impulsive decision. During grief, one must take one's time. Don't rush important decisions. Think about it. Talk about it. And give it some time. Counseling made me appreciate the importance of conversation and thought.

Throughout our grieving process, I have been careful to try to take my time, and it has paid off. It is difficult to think of too many situations where I have rushed into something and caused a mistake. I can't emphasize it enough: *Take your time.*

The other benefit to counseling was that I learned that I was heading in the right direction with my children. I had the right instincts, and I did understand my children and what they were going through as individuals. I knew their personalities and I was reading their behaviors correctly. I realized that there was no special formula to coping with grief. It's all about knowing your children, being a good parent, trial and error, and being there for them. It's about routine, love,

honesty, and security. Those are four simple essentials I return to over and over again as I guide my children through
grief, and I'll explore each one of them in the next part of
the book.

How Children Experience Fear

When my husband was killed very suddenly in a seemingly
very safe place, one of my children would go into a panic at
school thinking that I was in trouble somehow. Quite a number of times, I would receive a call on my cell phone asking
me where I was and what all the strange noises in the back-
ground were. He never asked me if I was in danger, he just
needed to hear my voice and find out exactly where I was
and what I was doing. The "reason" for his call was that he
didn't feel well, and he would then claim to have a stomachache or other physical ailment. The school was very ac-
commodating to my son's needs and never prohibited him
from reaching out to me, although I'm sure they were well
aware that he wasn't actually ill. Only occasionally did he
call from the nurse's office.

   To calm Matthew's fears, I needed to speak with him
very reassuringly and tell him I was all right and merely at a
noisy restaurant with some of my girlfriends, or some other
such place. I'd also let him know that I wasn't too far away.
Of course, I would always offer to come to school and pick
him up, but after a lengthy conversation and many reassurances, he would tell me that he could make it through the
day. He would tell me that he was feeling better.

There was no pattern to his calls. They would come any time of day and on any day of the week. Sometimes as Matthew went off to school, I would think that he was fine, but then that seemed to be the day that I received the call. It stressed me out knowing that he was so anxious. All day, every day, I would wonder and worry that he was troubled. I was afraid to go too far away, and I was afraid of what he might do if he couldn't get in touch with me or if I couldn't get back to him in time if he were having a crisis. I was afraid to be too far away because of my own fears, too. I needed to feel that I could get to him quickly, just as much as he needed to be reassured of my proximity. In the end, he just needed to know that I was okay and nearby for him. He was scared.

Physical ailments are a very common problem among children suffering grief, and such ailments often surface from emotional stress, including fear. Children may not want to go to school one day because perhaps they are feeling afraid. They are afraid, too, that as a parent, you will not let them miss a day of school. Rather than confront this emotional issue, they feel real, physical pain.

On occasion, Ian or Matthew wouldn't want to go to school. Sometimes it was a stomachache; sometimes it was a general "I don't feel well." Never did my sons admit to feeling sad or afraid. Never did they confront their emotions. I don't think they realized it had anything to do with their emotions.

I did allow them to miss school when they really didn't feel up to it, but I would warn them that unless they were clearly ill, they would have to be dragged around with me. I still had errands to run and I still needed to go to the gym to lessen my stress. The school was aware of the situation and left it totally up to my discretion. Other than offering support, I didn't feel the teachers could assist me. Whether or not the school trusted my judgment, I knew my children better than anyone and I was ultimately responsible for their well-being. But missing school wasn't anything exciting for my kids, and, in fact, it was boring. Still, they needed to be with me so I let them, at least for a while.

My daughter found refuge in school and she always wanted to go. She even chose to go back to school a day earlier than I had suggested because it seemed more logical to her. I had told my children that the Monday following the memorial service was to be when they needed to return to school. Emma, however, decided that she was going to try it on Friday, the day before the service. When I asked her why she wanted to go that day, she told me she wanted to try it for one day and then use the weekend to regroup before starting with a full week. I was so impressed. I had never even thought of that. Emma knew what she needed better than I did. Your child may know what is best for him or her. I didn't always have the answers, and you might not. Sometimes a child does. (I'll discuss the issue of school attendance more in an upcoming chapter, "Routine.")

Don't discount a child's fear, but instead try to comfort him or her. Use your instincts and do what feels right given the situation. Don't forget, if you are grieving, too, there may be days when you can't face the world. Treat a child as you might treat yourself. Children need guidance and boundaries.

Fear, like guilt and anger, will come and go. One child might call from school to check up on you, and then after a couple months never need to do it again. Another child may never call from school and then six months later panic when you are out to dinner one night and call you four times during the meal, then stay awake for hours when you don't appear at the appointed time, fearing something terrible has happened.

Fear of abandonment can be tremendous. A sudden trip to the emergency room by a parent for a tetanus shot or a visit to the doctor's office for a headache can cause irrational panic in a child. The child's fear may suddenly noticeably increase as he or she worries your injury could somehow be life threatening. Life has already upset the grieving child enough; the illness or injury of a single parent may cause a child to become afraid of facing death and insecurity again.

Ian seemed to be displaying his grief in a very open way. I felt that I had a handle on it. Boy, was I wrong. One night, about six months after David died, I was at a nearby restaurant with some girlfriends. Ian kept calling me with silly questions, such as could he have a snack; what time was I coming home; and what were we doing tomorrow? He was really acting out at home and driving his siblings nuts. Then, he wouldn't go to bed and kept fooling around. When I told him that I would be home soon, it didn't help. He wanted me home immediately. I told him that I needed some fun sometimes, too, and while he gets his time, I should get mine. But

I let him know that I would be home in about thirty minutes. I actually returned home about one hour later. Emma was still awake because Ian was so distressed that something had happened to me. Ian was so worried that he was unable to settle down and to go to sleep. I never imagined his fears would emerge suddenly. This wasn't the first time that I had left him and gone out to dinner. Why, now, was he feeling so anxious?

Around that same time, I went out to a birthday party. It was an evening filled with dancing and fun. Unfortunately, I injured my toe while I was dancing shoeless, and I had to be taken to the emergency room to have it treated. When I got home, the children were in bed asleep. It wasn't until the next morning, as I hobbled into the television room on crutches and recounted the amusing story to my children, complete with funny details about the party and all the teasing I'd endured over my trip to the ER, that to my surprise, Ian became incredibly upset. He began crying, worried that I had been to the hospital and was now on crutches. I assured him I was fine, but it made me realize just how fragile my children were. Though they all expressed their feelings differently, Emma, Ian, and Matthew were terrified of me leaving them, too.

Some children may be so angry, guilty, confused, or overwhelmed, that they have a hard time handling their fear. A simple phone call from a soothing mother or father doesn't help. They may act out in school, trying to draw attention to themselves. You may have an experience where your child may start physical fights with his or her family or friends, or try to control her life by not eating meals. Children may do all of these things because they are afraid and looking for solutions. They are trying to recapture some control in their lives because the death has made them feel insecure and out of control.

One of my first difficult experiences with Ian came quite early on after David died. Ian refused to eat his dinner. He would come down to the table and just sit there, impervious to my pleading and cajoling. I was already under enough stress, and now I had a child who wouldn't eat and seemed determined to starve himself. I became quite frantic. After a couple of evenings of me begging him and him keeping his mouth and arms tightly closed, I gave up. I ignored him and told him that he must at least drink his milk. Maybe even I'd let him have a cookie or two if he wanted it. Eventually, hunger and lack of interest from all parties got the better of him, and quietly, he began to consume his food again. It was a huge relief.

I eventually realized that this was just his way of trying to control his environment. He was scared and he had no control over David's death, but not eating was something that he could control. He thought it would help him to cope. In this instance, I knew better.

Fears that existed before the death of a loved one can become exaggerated after a loss. My son Matthew has always had a fear of dogs, but after David died, Matthew's fear became out of control. Just seeing a dog would cause him to burst into fits of panic and terror. Dogs that Matthew had previously been comfortable around were suddenly terrifying him. Even talking about dogs would upset Matthew. Rather than ignore his fear or push him into an uncomfortable position, I tried to remain sensitive to Matthew's worries while carrying on with our daily activities. I worked on helping Matthew by slowly and patiently introducing him into situations with familiar dogs in the security of my protection. It has taken a long time, but Matthew has grown less frightened. He is back to where he was prior to his dad's death.

As a parent, it is up to you to recognize a child's fear or anxiety and to try to address it. You know your child better than anyone, and your child relies on you more than anyone. Unlike Matthew, Ian became temporarily terrified of the dark, and he needed to keep his light burning all night. This fear was easier to address than Matthew's irrational fear of dogs. I had no problem allowing him to keep his light on, and since Ian didn't share a room with a sibling, his request affected nobody else. The light made Ian feel more secure, he was able to sleep, and it lessened some of his fear.

It is a caregiver's responsibility to make a child feel as secure as you possibly can. Giving your child a stable routine, a lot of love, and sincere honesty will all contribute to his or her sense of security. As a caregiver, grief cannot be selfish. The process is exhausting and challenging, but so rewarding when you see your child healing. It strengthens your resolve.

Taking Care of Yourself—So That You Can Take Care of Your Child

There are times when it is important for a caregiver to have a break, to get away from his or her children. Although I love my children very much, I need to get away at times.

When I feel overwhelmed or exhausted, I know that the best way for me to help my children is to pull myself together. I can't do that when I'm surrounded by my children's needs. Even if it's just for a couple of hours, that time alone helps me to be a better parent to my children. When I get my time alone, I love my children rather than resent them.

Tell your children, just as they need some quiet time, so do you. However, make sure that they can always get in touch with you. Keep a cell phone with you at all times so they can contact you if they suddenly feel panicky. Also, try not to travel too far away, so in the event of a crisis, you can reach them quickly. It will lessen their fears if they know you are nearby and readily accessible.

A support group was one of the first places I escaped to after David was killed. The group met every Tuesday night, and I made it a part of my routine. Initially, friends would come over to watch the children during the two hours that I was away, and then I found a teacher to step in. It was helpful to me not only as an individual but also as a parent. Listening to other parents and their struggles with their children's grief clarified and enhanced my understanding of this terrible and draining process. I was able to hear and discuss various situations that I had already dealt with or might encounter in the future. It was very beneficial to know others were suffering and struggling, all trying to move in the same positive direction. Through unity, grief and fear can be lessened and one can gain more strength.

I kept my cell phone on at all times during the support group meetings, and the children knew that I was only a ten-minute car ride away. Also, they felt comfortable with their caregivers. They knew them well. If I couldn't leave my children at home, then I would always bring them to someone's home that they had been to before, so that they had a certain level of comfort with their surroundings.

Naturally, there were times when it was impossible for me to leave them. If one of them wasn't feeling well or if something else pressing arose, I would stay home. But it was such a wonderful tonic for me to get out of the house and to have a break. Not to have to worry about helping them with their homework or getting them to bed enabled me to recharge my batteries and to have the strength to carry on. I really looked forward to that break, and when the support group ended, I held on to my caregiver for one evening a week and continued to use the time to get out and treat myself to some time to attend to my needs. Going to the movies or out to dinner with a friend was something for me to look forward to when I was feeling overwhelmed. It also gave me some adult conversation and emotional support. The children adjusted and accepted it into our new routine. I was a better mother for it.

✦

We talk about David daily. Sometimes it is something funny. Sometimes it is something annoying. Sometimes it is just something that reminds us of him and we want to share it. It took my children a while to talk about their dad. I made a point of doing it from the word *go*. Even if they couldn't speak it, they were constantly going to hear his name from me. I wasn't going to let his ghost fade into the back of our troubled minds.

After about three months, they all began to say his name in conversation. And what was even nicer was that they weren't even consciously aware they were doing it. It just became natural. It took them a while, but we got there and I wasn't going to let it drop until we did. It's important to help children learn to live with the memory and not to be afraid. They must learn to say the name of their loved one. You may find that your child is able to do this quickly or it may take your child a very long time, but ultimately, when a child is able to do this, it will help in the grieving process.

Children may have a fear of forgetting a loved one, and they may also be too ashamed to acknowledge that fear. Help them to overcome this fear by keeping the memory alive for them. You may want to place a picture of the loved one by a child's bed or talk to your child about the loved one daily. Let your child know that although this person is dead, that person can still be a part of his or her life. Try to discuss and take joy in the memories.

Let children know that you are afraid as well. Tell them that you are having a hard time helping them through their grief. It is frightening because it is painful and uncertain. It is scary because even as an adult you cannot give them all the answers for which they are searching. Your job as a caregiver is to help to guide them through these fears and their grief. Your job as a caregiver is to give them routine, love, honesty, and security.

What You Can Do to Help
Your Child Confront Fear

- Every child will have some sort of fear, and it will manifest itself in a variety of ways.
- A parent or guardian should consider attending counseling or joining a support group, if only to help determine how to guide a child. It will lessen anxiety for all involved.
- Fear can lead to impulsive, improper choices. Take your time when making decisions.
- Be accessible. Carrying a cell phone or beeper will allow a child to contact you at all times and lessen a child's fear.
- Initially, try not to travel too far away. Let a child know that you can reach him or her quickly if you are needed.
- Fear causes stress that can manifest itself physically. Be sensitive to a child's physical complaints.
- School can lessen or increase a child's fear. Pay attention to your child's feelings toward school, and be patient.

- Fear may cause a change in behavior, such as bullying, emotional outbursts, or a need for control.
- Within reason, be honest about your own fears. Demonstrate to the child that you are trying to overcome these challenges as life goes on.
- Always try to leave your child with a familiar face when using a babysitter.
- Don't let your child's fears immobilize you. Do what needs to be done for a child and stay in control.
- Previous fears can become more exaggerated, or new fears may develop, such as a fear of the dark or animals.
- Be tolerant and patient of seemingly irrational fears. Time will heal as a child feels more secure. If concerned, consult a counselor.
- Talk about the lost loved one and keep the memory alive. Initiate conversation and take pleasure from the memories.
- The best way for a child to overcome fear is through routine, love, honesty, and security.

PART THREE

GUIDING A CHILD
THROUGH LOSS

With
Routine, Love,
Honesty, and Security

Routine

After my husband died, the first two questions my children asked me when we were alone together and it had quieted down were was I going to remarry and was I going to have to get a job. At first I was horrified that they were looking to replace their father, but after I had time to reflect, I realized that they couldn't imagine this new life. They were desperately trying to undo what had been done and replacement seemed to be the most immediate solution. They told me that they wanted me to remarry because they wanted a dad again. They wanted life to be normal again. They wanted the same routine as always.

Just as intensely, I wanted them to have a father again, to have the same routine and normal life, but as an adult I knew replacement wouldn't suddenly make things all better. We would have to learn to adjust to a new and different "normal."

The second question about whether I was going to have to get a job made them equally as concerned, as I had always been a stay-at-home mother. That day, they had their world ripped out from under their feet. Life had metamorphosed into something they no longer understood. Now that they no longer had the security of two loving parents, were their lives also going to be changed by day care or some stranger taking care of them? Could I cope, financially and otherwise, with them alone?

I knew that what they needed in this time of crisis was security, and security came in part through routine. I needed to keep the routine the same as it had been prior to their father's death. Perhaps three months or two years from now, I would be working. But for the immediate future, I would be with them in the same way as always. Their lives were not going to change any more than they already had. I was going to do everything in my power to keep the routine as similar to the way it had been.

Understandably, some things were bound to change. We needed to discover a new "normal." Every evening before David's death, I would feed the children their dinner and after putting them to bed, David and I would sit down to our meal. Now that David had died, our old routine would certainly have to change. Rather than eating with David, I now had two choices: I could start a new routine of eating with the children or I could eat alone. I immediately began to eat with the children. For the children, that adjustment was not very big because I would always sit with them when they ate their dinner. It was my own routine that altered significantly in that instance.

So although some changes will inevitably alter a past routine, most things for us, such as schedules, stayed the same because I allowed them to. I wanted my children to feel as if they had something to hold on to that they understood and expected. They needed to have some security in their daily lives. I didn't want to increase their fear. A lot can happen in a few months. Grief moves on and hopefully children heal. Maybe six months from now my children would want me to go to work. But for now, they needed to hear that our lives would stay the same. I needed to be strong and remain a constant to them.

We had many people bringing dinner and food over to the house. I was so consumed with the necessary paperwork surrounding David's death and attending to my children's needs, that it was a relief for me not to have to cook. It was very hard for me to focus on anything outside of that bubble and the thought of going to the supermarket terrified me. I could only imagine what it would be like for my children to return to school. It wasn't the actual shopping that worried me. It was bumping into people and having to talk about how I felt, or how the children were, that I didn't want to deal with. No wonder my kids were reluctant to return to school or to have any attention drawn to them. Studying, homework, and staring eyes would be a lot for them to handle. For me, I wasn't too sure that I would have the strength and concentration required by merely tackling food shopping.

I recall the first time I ventured out to the market alone, a couple of months after David's death. I walked very quickly with my eyes pointing down all the time, so that I could avoid any confrontation. It wasn't an enjoyable experience, but I did it and the next time it was a little easier.

Although it was great for me to not have to expend the energy to cook and to use that energy focusing on my children and myself, Emma, Ian, and Matthew soon grew very tired of delivered meals. Every night, they were unhappy with the meal that had been delivered. They complained constantly, and there was always one who was so unhappy that he or she was close to tears.

After a while, I decided that once a week I would take them to the drive-through at a fast-food restaurant so that they could order what they wanted. Then we would all sit down at the kitchen table and happily talk about life while they devoured a familiar meal. It made a big difference getting drive-through that one day each week. It gave the children familiarity, but it also gave them choice. They got to choose what type of food and what type of meal they wanted that evening. They now had something to look forward to and it gave them a little bit of control, which helped them to feel a little more secure.

But ultimately, what the children really wanted was the familiarity of Mom's cooking. It is a real balancing act trying to juggle between what is right for one's children and what a caregiver is capable of giving during times of grief. I knew that my children wanted me to cook them their dinner, but I didn't have the strength to do it. I needed time to heal as well. But the fact was, my children were relying on me to help them to heal, and Mom's cooking made them feel a lot happier. I explained that although I knew they were upset and stressed to find an unusual meal in front of them each night, I needed a little more time before I could cook for them. Grief has its own road map. I asked my children to be patient and travel this path with me for just a little while, until a new road opened up for us. Eventually, it would benefit us all.

Then finally, one evening when a mystery meal appeared on our doorstep and I called my children down to dinner, they came down, looked at it, and all started crying. They just wanted Mom's cooking and they wanted dinner to taste normal. They didn't want anyone else's pasta or meatloaf. They wanted the delivered meals to stop. They had had enough.

I knew that at this point I needed to start cooking again. It didn't have to be anything complicated or fancy. It just needed to be from me. My children clearly let me know that they needed the routine of familiar foods, and they needed to see me in my role as their mother doing what I had done as their mother before their dad died. They needed that little bit of security.

So I returned to my routine of weekly shopping trips to various food stores, and got out my dusty pans and made their favorite simple meals. How happy they were! I kept it

simple for a while, but the routine of cooking again and doing life's daily errands was good for me, too. By helping my
children adjust back to routine, they helped me. Life goes on.

It is difficult to know when the "right time" is for doing
something. Each family deals with grief in its own way. The
right time for me to begin cooking again might have been the
wrong time for another family. It is a different path for
everyone, whether it's cooking, going back to work or
school, or resuming any part of your previous routine that
you've put "on hold" during your grieving process. You
should try not to feel pressured about your choices, and try
to ignore others who may pass judgment on your choices.
Everyone has different issues and different fears. Listen to
your children and listen to your gut and make a choice that
feels right *for you and your family*. Don't be afraid to take
your time and never rush yourself or your child into anything. Listen to what signals a child is giving you and think
about it. The answer was always easiest for me when I gave
myself some time. It is easy to feel panicky about choices and
to question your decisions, especially when other people
might not agree with your choices. But remember that you
know your children better than anyone else. Never let anyone pressure you into something that you don't feel is right
for your children. You know what upsets them, what pleases
them, what scares them, and what makes them feel loved. Do
what you can do to lessen their worries and to add to their
happiness, keeping in mind that you may make mistakes. No
one has the perfect trail map for navigating through grief,
even those who have lived through it.

Another routine that was difficult was school. I decided that I didn't want my children to go back to school until after the memorial service, which was a week and a half after their father had been killed. Up until the service, I wanted to be together as a family, just in case they suddenly needed me or I needed them. I wanted to be there for them every second to reassure them and to love them. Also, selfishly, I didn't quite have the energy to be getting up early every morning, making their lunch, and driving them to school. I wasn't ready for that routine yet.

I called the schools to let them know what my children and I had decided about their return. Both the elementary and the middle schools sent over their guidance counselors to speak with my kids. None of my children wanted to say much, but they all felt very strongly about one point: When they returned to school, they wanted it to be normal. They didn't want other children talking to them about their father or their feelings. They wanted to be treated just the same as every other student and not to be singled out. School for them needed to be a refuge. A place where they could still feel secure, happy, and normal. A place where the routine hadn't altered since September 11 and they knew what to expect. For them, when they were at school, they wanted the break from their reality at home.

Quite a few months after David died, we were all sitting at the kitchen table eating dinner when Matthew asked me where I felt the safest. It was a very strange question for me because I didn't feel particularly safe anywhere at this point in my life, but I thought about my answer. After a few moments, I told him that I would have to choose my bed. It was always warm, inviting, and comfortable. Ian and Emma couldn't come up with an answer at the moment but Ian later told me that he felt safest around me. Matthew was bursting to declare his spot of safety. Surprisingly to me, he told us that he felt safest at school.

The schools knew how important they were to my children and they were very good about listening to my children's wishes of wanting to be treated normally. They made an announcement in the elementary school letting the other students know my sons' request. In the middle school the teachers informed my daughter's classmates of her needs in a more intimate environment, discussing it within her individual classes.

Both ways worked out fine, and my children found the return of school days to be a welcome return to normalcy. Of course, as I mentioned earlier, there were some days after that when my children didn't want to go to school. It was never Emma wanting to stay home, but the boys commonly had an excuse. Some days it would be a stomachache, whereas other days it would be just that they weren't feeling well. They never came right out and said that they didn't want to go to school because they were upset. I don't think they even knew why they didn't want to go to school that particular day. They just didn't and that was fine with me. Some days they just needed to be alone with Mom and have some quiet time.

As a mother, I had to use my judgment and try to gauge when it was okay to stay home. Too often at home, and I would have a problem. It wasn't always easy to know when they needed me and when they just felt like missing school because they were normal kids trying to think of excuses for staying home. I couldn't let them manipulate me and turn their grief into a crutch. Sometimes I had to take a hard line that left me feeling upset, but knowing in my heart that it was the right thing to do for them. I made sure that the school had my phone numbers and that I was always accessible in the event one of my children needed me. Still, I didn't want to send them to school when they really couldn't face it. I had to try to assess their pain on each and every day. As a caregiver, you need to listen to your instincts and trust them. Put yourself in the shoes of the child and imagine how you would feel, remembering that we all must do things that we would rather not in order to heal.

Homework was another issue. Now that they were back into the routine of school, how far did I push with homework? That was something else that I discussed with the teachers. I knew that I wasn't able to concentrate on anything. How were my children supposed to do it? I talked with Emma, Ian, and Matthew about it and let them know that it was all right if they didn't feel like doing their homework some nights, but that I expected them to try when they felt up to it. If they wanted to be treated normally at school, then they needed to try to behave like normal schoolchildren, which meant having their homework completed when they could manage it.

The guidance counselors at school also told them the same thing, and told them that they would speak with their teachers about it. But just getting back into the routine of school and not having their dad around was a big enough adjustment for all of us at the moment. The focus and discipline of a homework routine could come later. I didn't have the energy to oversee their homework assignments anyway. They were smart kids and I knew they would catch up quickly. Although I didn't tell the children, I wasn't worried and, frankly, homework seemed the least of my worries.

After what I had felt was enough time, I started expecting more of the children regarding their homework. I worried about them developing bad study habits. In the late fall, I told them that after the Christmas break I expected them to be more conscientious about their homework. They needed to start getting it done, on a regular basis. By telling them ahead of time, I gave them a lot of time to get prepared. Also, I made sure that these new expectations would be enforced after the holidays so that they could be rested and more focused. I reminded them often about my anticipation that soon they would have to be more responsible. Using grief as a crutch is not helping healing to progress.

So come January, they were back into a completely normal school routine, homework and all. Still, there were times when they didn't get their homework done, but they knew that I expected them to try, and that they had to come up with a pretty good excuse as to why it wasn't completed.

The majority of the time, it was Ian and Matthew who gave me a hard time about their homework. Although they were much better after the holidays and did make efforts to complete their assignments, it wasn't until the following school year that they really got back into a good study routine. Ian even took a little longer than that, closer to a year and a half. Fortunately, they were only in fifth grade, not in high school.

Emma generally always completed her assignments, even upon first returning to school in September. She was in seventh grade and she was concerned about falling behind and getting bad grades. I was actually more concerned about Emma's stress level when she didn't have the energy or focus to complete her homework on occasion. She would cry and get very distraught about getting into trouble because her homework wasn't done. I would endlessly try to reassure her that it was all right, but she couldn't be convinced. Eventually, I had to go into the school and ask the teachers to speak with her on an individual basis, so that she knew it was fine with all of them if she came to class empty-handed some mornings.

I thought that I was making it easier for my children by not forcing them to do their homework, but for Emma it caused her more stress. She was desperately trying to hold on to a routine that she didn't always have the energy to do. In the end, not having the pressure to always get her homework done did help. But it took us a little while to find the right formula with which she felt comfortable. I should have discussed it with my children a bit more before moving forward in what I thought was the best way to handle it.

Routines are so important to the welfare of children. It gives them the stability and security that they crave. Don't feel like you have to push them back into a totally normal routine immediately after a death of a loved one, but don't be afraid of routine, either. If they're in a routine, chances are you will be, too. It helps them to see you living your life just as you always have. It takes away some of their fear. It will take away some of your fear, too, because your children will feel and act more contented.

One routine that Emma wasn't ready to begin again was her soccer. Going back was going to be extremely difficult. Her father had been her soccer coach her entire life. Now he was gone and soccer only reinforced that absence. Frankly, I wasn't sure how to handle it, though I thought the exercise would alleviate some of her stress. In addition, many of her closest friends were on her soccer team and the emotional support from them was huge.

All of her teammates had been severely affected by David's death. He had been their coach for many years as well. These girls had come to know him and to care about him. Whenever any girl became injured or upset at practice or a game, David had always made a point of calling the child that evening to make sure she was all right. Sometimes he knew the outburst was for preteen, emotional reasons, but he weighed that just as equally as an injury and called them regardless. For this and many other reasons, David had been a wonderfully supportive, kind, and caring coach and it pained most of the girls to return to soccer. Seated together and dressed in uniform, they had all come to his memorial service. They had compiled a booklet of their individual memories about him for the service, which David's assistant coach read aloud. It was a very moving tribute to his memory and to his abilities as a coach. He was truly loved.

Given how fond Emma's teammates were of David, they were highly concerned about her well-being. I thought their concern for her would help her and that she would find some support in returning to soccer.

I continually pressured her into returning to practice. Mentally, I compared it to falling off a horse. Jump back on before it all seems too intimidating and it strips you of the power to return. I was worried that if she didn't go back to soccer now, she might never do it again. Knowing how much both she and her father loved the game, I was worried.

Repeatedly, Emma resisted my pleas, saying that she wasn't ready. Finally, she acquiesced. I gave her my phone and told her to call me if she had any problems. The field was only a two-minute drive away. Well, when the call came, my heart sank. She was crying hysterically, telling me that she couldn't do it. I felt so terrible. I felt responsible for causing her additional pain and torment. Why had I pushed her into this? Why hadn't I listened to her worries more? Why didn't I put myself in her shoes?

As a caregiver, mistakes will be made. After I picked up Emma, I hugged her and apologized for my error. She was mad at me for putting her through more pain. I didn't blame her. I told her that I had pushed her too soon, so now, I wouldn't make her return until she decided that she was ready.

The coach called to talk with me about it. He was understandably concerned. I told him that I didn't know when Emma would return to soccer. Maybe she never would. I would have to let her take some time and figure it out for herself. She needed to heal a bit more first so that she had the strength to face running out onto the soccer field.

It wasn't until I had to return to the soccer field myself that I realized just how painful the experience must have been for Emma. Ian and Matthew also played soccer, and David had been their coach for a few years. After a couple of years, however, David realized that coaching two teams was too difficult, so he carried on solely with Emma's team. Because Emma was averse to playing soccer again, I thought perhaps the boys would be hesitant. Not the case. They were eager to return to the field and to run off their energy. When it came time for Ian and Matthew's first game, naturally I knew that I had to be there to watch them. Either David or I had always gone to their games and I wasn't going to let them down now. They needed my support.

Walking onto that soccer field was one of my more challenging emotional experiences. This field was a complex of multiple fields where my husband had spent many hours. It represented something he loved. Also, there were crowds of spectators milling about at various fields and everyone seemed to stand still and stare as I walked across the long stretch of green to find my sons. Holding back tears and suppressing my anguish was taking every ounce of my resilience. I hadn't anticipated such turmoil.

It wasn't until I sat down and someone approached to ask me if I was okay that I burst into tears. I didn't want my sons to see how upset I was, so it was very difficult. Ian and Matthew were enjoying themselves and I didn't want to arouse their concern and distract them. Even if Emma and I couldn't get any pleasure from soccer, I wanted the boys to carry on enjoying it.

After that experience, I realized just how hard it must be for Emma to actually play soccer. Even though I didn't even really like the game, I was a wreck. Emma, who would eventually go back to playing soccer, had loved soccer and had spent every minute doing it with her father, so the memories would be overwhelming and her emotions powerful.

You may find that you or your children need to take your time, perhaps because one or both isn't emotionally ready, in restarting a particular routine, and that's okay. But let your child know that you will be restarting most routines in the future, and don't be afraid to talk about it with your child. Children need to know that parents have certain expectations of them. These expectations are important because through them children know that they are cared about and loved. However, make sure that your expectations are reasonable and consistent. Routines need consistency in order to be routines.

When your child's routine—restored at last—is broken for some reason, expect him or her to become upset, perhaps more so than usual. Routines will get broken and changes will happen. Halfway through the school year, Emma's seventh-grade English teacher was suddenly fired. The children had no warning. One day the teacher was there, and the next day she was gone. Emma was devastated by the news.

She felt betrayed and angry. The school was her sanctuary, a place of familiar routine and anticipated security.

Emma doesn't share her feelings very easily. She had to keep a journal for this English class and she had exposed herself with some pretty honest emotion. She felt she had shared her soul with this teacher through her writing, and now suddenly, the teacher was gone. Emma had taken a risk by trusting her and now she felt vulnerable.

Emma realized that it wasn't the teacher's fault, but it hurt nonetheless. She was so angry with the school. She cried hysterically for the better part of the day, and couldn't get through all of her classes, so the administration had to send her into the guidance counselor's office.

Once she was in the office, though, Emma had enough sense and honesty to realize that it wasn't all about her English teacher. It was really about her dad. She missed him. She needed him. She wanted him. She was angry and in pain, and she felt abandoned, overwhelmed by loss. This break in her academic routine had set off all sorts of emotions that she had been suppressing. Ultimately, I was relieved something had happened that unleashed such a torrent of emotion to flow out of Emma. I had been concerned that she had been too "together" lately and that she hadn't displayed enough emotion about her father. Nonetheless, it was very stressful and upsetting for everyone involved at the time. It took a lot of time for Emma to readjust to school.

Sometimes, an unexpected event will send your hardest efforts into reverse. All that you can do as a caregiver is to listen to your gut and do what you think is right. Follow routines, but don't feel that once you have made a decision, you can't go back on it. Days change, feelings change, life changes. Sometimes when you feel like you have one area of your life under control, something traumatic will occur and change everything.

Be flexible. Sometimes I have days when I feel like doing nothing. So, too, will your child. Be sensitive to that without being too protective. Protecting them from their grief doesn't help them to get over it. They need to have some bad days just as you do. They will have days when they don't want any routine. It's okay. A routine is there to go back to. They need to get through the grieving process alone, in their own way. You can support them, but you can't grieve for them.

One routine that I really pushed the boys into continuing was their piano lessons. David loved music and particularly the piano. He had always desperately wanted to learn to play the piano, so for his fortieth birthday I gave him a year's worth of piano lessons. He loved playing and practicing. It helped to relieve his stress. Early weekend mornings or weekday evenings, David would sit down and play. My children and I all became familiar with his repertoire and his stumbling points. His routine had become welcoming and comforting to us.

After David's death, I really wanted the boys to continue playing for David's sake. They are very good musically and they had made quite a lot of progress on the piano. I didn't want to let David down by not staying on top of their lessons. He took great pride in the boys' talents and accomplishments on the piano. He really loved it.

But Ian and Matthew had other ideas. They couldn't get back into their love of piano. It became a struggle for them and the practicing came to a halt. When the teacher would arrive for lessons, the boys would cry and refuse to come down. I found it all very difficult and stressful. Clearly, they had no desire to play at the moment, but I felt guilt over not having them play for their father.

I finally decided to let them have a break for a while. I was hoping to give them time to readjust. Maybe they would start to miss playing the piano and return willingly. Even the piano teacher said that he had noticed a big change since their father had died and that maybe they needed a vacation from it.

With a heavy heart, I agreed to let them stop playing. It was so difficult because I knew how disappointed David would have been. But at the same time, I could see the anguish it was causing my sons. Ian and Matthew were so relieved to be able to quit, and it was more than one year before they wandered over to the piano to play. Interestingly, a year and a half after David's death, Matthew started showing a sudden and intense interest in playing the piano again. He would sit down and play for over an hour as he tried to recall his pieces. After a couple days, I decided to ask him if he would like to have piano lessons again. He said that he would think about it. I didn't push it because I didn't want him to feel pressured. However, the next day, he told me that he did want to begin lessons again. I was thrilled and found him a teacher quickly. It was so wonderful to hear him getting pleasure from an instrument that he had learned to love again. David's wishes were once more alive.

Now both boys will talk about the music their father played, and, together, we joke about his imperfections on the instrument. They smile when they hear a song he played, remembering their father, and taking comfort in the memory of their dad's old routine.

The holidays are extremely difficult. Many times, families have had routines or traditions in place for many years when it comes to holiday time. Trying to do something different, while still remembering the loved one and having it feel like a holiday, is very hard.

Thanksgiving and Christmas fell only a few months after David died. I didn't even know what I wanted to do, so how could I even begin to guess what the children wanted? I did speak with them about it and gave them a couple of ideas and options. I felt that we had to do something just a little bit different; however, the children loved our routines and wanted things to be the same. I don't think that they had the maturity to project and to understand the difficulties of celebrating the holidays exactly as we always had.

Not wanting to stress them out in advance but also not wanting to cause additional problems during the holidays, I decided to compromise. For Thanksgiving, we had always gone to Vermont. We would do the same this year except that we would stay somewhere else. For Christmas, we would still stay at home for the morning and carry on with our traditions until mealtime. Then we would spend the afternoon doing something different.

For both holidays, I felt that I needed to be surrounded by friends or family. Although I think that our adjustments did make it a little easier, in the end I'm not sure that it mattered that much. It was really hard.

My daughter seemed to cope okay. She kept herself busy and tried to make the most of things, looking for humor where she could find it. My sons, on the other hand, were terrible. They never actually said that they were upset or that they were having a difficult time. They just acted out like crazy. They cried. They refused to eat. They didn't want to cooperate. They just wanted to go sit somewhere alone and cry or throw things against the wall. They were very angry and distressed. I tried to comfort them, but it was close to impossible. They were hurting. I was hurting. Honestly, I didn't have the energy or the interest, and I had to do what I could for myself to get through the holidays, too. So, I gave them what attention I could and let them be.

I realized that my children just needed to make it through those holidays in the way that was best for them. If I had been crying and angry all day, no one would have tried to change my behavior, so I didn't change theirs. Neither holiday was a particularly positive or easy one, but we did make it through, and by the end of the "celebrations," we were still in one piece. I just made sure that I gave them all extra-big hugs those nights.

As time goes on, I'm sure the holidays will become easier. We decided to go away just before our second Christmas without David. My family was having a get-together down in Florida to celebrate a beloved friend's eightieth birthday. The friend, Dorothy, is a lovely German woman who helped my mother to take care of my six siblings and me while we were growing up. She is like a second grandmother to us.

Dorothy's party was the Sunday before Christmas, so I decided to go down to Florida early, and take the children to Disney World. We hadn't flown since David had been killed but I felt now was the time. We were ready.

The children were very excited about going to Disney, but we did have reservations, too. As a family, we had been to Disney once before with David, in September 1999. We had had a wonderful time together, and we had very fresh and powerful memories. Would our return cause us further anguish? Would too many memories come flashing back and get us depressed? I was very concerned about it, but I hadn't yet voiced my worries. Then one evening, Matthew brought it up at dinner. He said that he was a little bit worried about going because the last time that we were in Disney was with Dad. I told him that I had the same trepidations but that I thought we should go. It was time to reintroduce the routine of vacations and it would be nice to be a family on vacation again. We could focus on the positive feelings that arose from our time with David, and besides, I told him, your father would want us to go, and he may still be with us, only in a different form.

It turned out to be a great holiday. Emma, who was not particularly enthusiastic about going, openly admitted that she had a wonderful time. I made sure that we stayed in a different hotel and that our agenda was slightly different. Also, after a few days, my children met up with their cousins and I spent time with some of my siblings, so that gave us emotional support and added to the difference.

But we thought about David a lot. Before or after almost every ride at the park, one of us would comment on David's like or dislike of that particular ride and our memories of experiencing that ride with him. It was a very positive thing for all of us, and it made the vacation even that much more special. It made us feel good about David and what we had shared with him. It was a very significant step in our grieving process. It was healing.

In addition to our unexpected healing, the vacation brought relief from the holidays to me. The anticipation of a holiday can sometimes be worse than the day itself, and being removed from that stress helped me relax.

We returned home on the evening of December 23 and Christmas was upon us. We spent Christmas Eve and Christmas Day with friends doing some of the old routine and some of last year's new routine. We were developing a new way of marking the holidays. We felt rested and happy from our time away together and Christmas turned out to be quite an enjoyable day. Without expecting it, and without thought toward our future, we seem to have found a new routine that worked for us.

Going away sometime over the Christmas holiday is a new tradition that I would like our family to continue. It helps me to look forward to our next Christmas together and it is a distraction from our old routine.

Without a doubt, routine has helped our family to endure and to make strides toward happiness and healing. It has been something for my children to cling on to during their times of uncertainty and confusion. As a caregiver, you should never underestimate the power of routine.

What You Can Do
to Guide Your Child with Routine

- Routine is a powerful tool for combating grief.
- Routine heals.
- After a loss, hold on to some routines such as mealtimes and bedtimes.
- Slowly reestablish old routines or introduce new routines, as both you and your child feel ready.
- Routines involving togetherness, such as family meals, board games, or outdoor activities, are strengthening. Initiate a Family Fun Night.
- Treat your child to a weekly or monthly pleasure. Buying ice cream, ordering out, or going to the movies are all welcome ideas for children.
- Help a child to develop his or her own routine with daily chores. Feeding a pet or making a bed gives a child responsibility with a scheduled obligation.
- Take your time with routine. Don't rush. Different routines will be introduced at different times among different families.
- Involve your child with deciding when to begin a routine, but don't give a child total control. You are the parent. You know your child. Trust your instincts.

- Have flexibility with your routines and don't be afraid to change routines.
- Routines need consistency in order to be routines.
- Familiarity of routines gives a child security.
- Don't be selfish when establishing routine.
- Some routines will need to be introduced in stages. Returning to school, music lessons, sports activities, and homework should all begin when a child is ready, and normally at differing times. Don't go from sitting at home doing nothing to a full, busy day. The stress may be too overwhelming for a child. Put yourself in the child's shoes.
- Routines, old and new, can be comforting.
- Don't fear routine.
- Developing new routines such as travel or reunions, especially around the holidays, can help in the healing process.
- Routine involves expectation. Following through on expectations brings about security. Security helps a child to heal.

Love

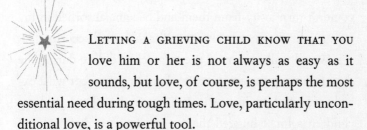

LETTING A GRIEVING CHILD KNOW THAT YOU love him or her is not always as easy as it sounds, but love, of course, is perhaps the most essential need during tough times. Love, particularly unconditional love, is a powerful tool.

During times of happiness and ease, love is sometimes taken for granted. We know that we love our children, but life can get so hectic and overwhelming, that sometimes we forget to show our love. You may remember when a lost temper or a missed conversation would occasionally come easier than a soft word or a hug. No parent is perfect. But children crave affection and reassurances, and telling them you love them from time to time is very important but not enough in itself. A parent needs to show a child by his or her actions, and those actions must be sincere because children are very perceptive, and they can be skeptical. So, hug your child. Listen to your child. Praise your child. Laugh with your child. And say "I love you." Do this with full attention on your child and be honest with your words and actions.

When I found out that David died, I went to the schools to pick up my children and to tell them about the terrible tragedy. I held them as tightly as I could while I told them the devastating news. I remember their anguish and disbelief as they stood or sat sobbing in my arms. They clutched on to me with all their strength hoping for protection.

At that point, I felt so completely powerless, but so determined to provide for them all the safety and comfort that I had the strength to give. I had to give them all my love. I couldn't turn away from them and become absorbed in my own grief. They needed my love for their own security.

We all walked around pretty much in a daze during the days following the accident. It's hard to remember what exactly was said or done. But I do remember that I held my children a lot. I hugged them a lot. I kissed them a lot. I praised them for their strength, and I told them how very much I loved them even more. I would say, "I'm so sorry about Dad. He loved you very much. We are going to really miss him. But I want you to know that I'm still your mother. I will always be your mother, and I will always be here for you. Anytime you want to talk or to have a hug, I'll be here. I love you so very much."

Sometimes it would be variations of those thoughts, but

whatever I said, I always followed it up with "I love you" and I always told them that I was there for them.

When a child is grieving, you can never tell them enough that you love them. If they start telling you that you are saying it too much, that's okay. Tell them you can't help yourself and that you won't say it in public to embarrass them. Blame it on your own grief. But tell them.

It is also important to back up your words with some actions. You should kiss them, hug them, and listen to them. Make sure that if you tell them that you are there for them, you really are there for them. Locking yourself in your bedroom, spending all your time with friends or other adults, or wanting to be alone all the time will quickly cause the child to doubt your sincerity.

As I've pointed out before, it is very difficult to be a caregiver during times of significant stress. It requires good parenting in an extreme situation. Children suffering from grief can be very demanding, leaving little time for your own needs, not to mention your own grieving process. These "extra" demands can vary daily and can range in intensity depending on the age and the personality of the child. You may have a grieving child who does not want to be alone at bedtime or during the night. Your child may suffer from nightmares or severe bed-wetting. A child who had not wet her bed in years may suddenly revert back to a bed-wetting pattern and you may find yourself having to get up and change sheets multiple times during the night. A child may want you to accompany him or her on every school field trip.

Personally, I chaperoned every school trip for all of my children during that first year after David's death. They wanted the security of my presence and I felt more comfortable being there for them. Of course, our family had the added trauma of fearing further terrorist attacks, so a trip into an unknown environment caused us additional stress; we did what we could to alleviate some of that stress. Families experiencing different types of loss may discover their own vulnerable situations.

In addition to the positive aspects of wanting attention, such as your child wanting you to accompany his class on a field trip, your child may also demand attention in negative ways. Acting out and misbehaving may be signs that your child needs you and is testing your limits to gauge your strength. Stay firm in your family value system and be consistent. The child will recognize that you are there for him. With all these new demands placed upon you as a caregiver, it will be hard to find any "alone time" or uninterrupted moments to deal with your own grief. But short-term, personal sacrifice will allow for greater freedom from a child's demands in the long run. Although exhausting, I often found the increased demands of my children to be a welcome distraction to my otherwise-empty moments.

Uncertainty on the part of the caregiver when disciplining a child is to be expected. Knowing what is right is never easy and a judgment call is a very personal decision. But, remember, if during times of grief your child acts out or behaves badly, it is all right to get angry with your child if his or her behavior is inappropriate. Just remind the child that it is his *behavior,* not him, that you are punishing or disappointed with. Let him know that you still love him, just not his behavior. And keep in mind that even though a death has altered your child's reality, children still need to have guidelines and boundaries. Anger during grief is to be expected, but beating up a brother to vent that anger is unacceptable. It was a very fine line for me to know what I should tolerate and what I shouldn't. Just like knowing the "right time" for something, acceptable behavior was also very difficult to define, especially in the beginning. I decided to rely on my instincts combined with my previous parenting expectations from when David had been alive. I tried to keep the rules the same, only with a more understanding, loving, and patient attitude. I basically remained consistent in our family value system, and my children got comfort from knowing what I expected of them. Love combined with routine and consistency is a very powerful tool when battling the demons of grief.

You will find that at times it will seem impossible to show your love for your child, as your child will act out, test and confuse you, and get angry with you. My daughter burst out crying one night saying that I didn't understand her and that the only one who did was her father. She said he was the only one she enjoyed being with and that her brothers and I drove her crazy. I was so angry. I was working so hard to protect her and to make her secure. I had pushed aside many of my own needs to accommodate her, and this was my thanks, an "I hate you."

I knew she was in pain and grieving terribly, but my own

pain was also intense and I didn't know if I had the energy to do battle. We both needed love. So, I took a big breath, sat down on her bed, and started crying. I told her that I was trying my best to be there for her but that it was hard for me, too. I knew that I couldn't fill her father's shoes but that she had to give me a chance and to cut me some slack. There was no manual for this type of situation and we all had to pull together to make it work. Then I told her that I loved her and I left the room.

About ten minutes later, after I had pulled myself together, I went back into her room, gave her a long hug, and told her how much I loved her. She just listened and didn't say a word. I know I broke through, and she seemed to understand what I was trying to tell her. Don't be afraid to admit to uncertainties to your child. It will let your child feel more comfortable in her uncertainties, as well.

I tell my children that no matter what happens in our lives, I will always love them. I might not approve of all their behavior but I will always love them, and so will their father.

A child may be feeling guilty or angry about the death of a loved one, as Emma was. Children may feel that the death was somehow their fault or related to their behavior in some way. It is important for children to know that you still love them, that you will always love them regardless of the person's death, and that you will reassure them that they have absolutely no reason to feel any guilt, if they are expressing concern. Their sense of guilt is something that they will have to get over in their own time, and this feeling usually goes away on its own. You cannot take away their negative, guilty feelings, but you can let them know that you still love them.

A child needs you to show love in different ways. Some children, such as my son Ian, might need you to listen to them and their fears every night for twenty minutes at bedtime. Others might want you to take them on a long walk, hold hands, and not say a word, while others, like my daughter, may sometimes just need you to come into their bedroom at night and silently hold them as they cry their heart out. Get to know your child and how he or she chooses to express his or her grief. Get to know what each needs from you given his or her individual personality. Each child will need love in a different way, but each will need it.

It is very normal to try to protect your grieving child from additional pain. When situations arise that cause your child to be distressed, such as when Emma's trusted English teacher was suddenly dismissed and she reacted so emotionally, it is very difficult to know how big a role one's grief plays in one's suffering. Is your child having this reaction because of his or her grief or is he just being himself, trying to adjust to life's normal challenges?

Before David died, my children had problems and stressful days. Now that he was gone, was I excusing them from everything and overprotecting them because of their grief? Was I allowing them to develop an excuse for all of their behavioral problems?

I decided that parenting through grief was different from my previous parenting only in that I would be more challenged. There was no guidebook for me. This was a test without any time to study. I had to fall back on the only knowledge that I had, which was my knowledge of being a good mother. Continuing to be a strong parent to my children was what they needed most. I knew I would face some extra-tough decisions, but I had to do what I felt was in their best interest, even if it was painful for any or all of us.

One such difficult decision was whether or not to send my children away for a short while to one of the 9/11 camps for kids, though nothing that I had come across felt right to me. I knew what they needed most was to be with other peers who were going through the same emotions they were experiencing, but I also wanted it to be a normal summer camp experience, somewhere that they could play and have fun, rather than sit around and talk about their feelings. I tried to get them to do enough "talking" at home. Also, I didn't want them to feel any pressure or to be put on the spot about being different. I wanted somewhere where they would bond with other children because the children were able to empathize with one another through their common experience of grief. Deeds, words, and actions would be tacitly understood, minus the psychoanalysis.

After searching and waiting, I finally came across a weeklong camp that was just what I was looking for. Designed for children in my kids' age group who'd lost a parent in the World Trade Center, it offered recreation, crafts, and other camp activities with absolutely no pressures placed on the children to discuss their emotions, though each cabin would have professionals for the campers to talk with should they want to. I called the camp and asked them to send me a video and any other information, and I told my children about it.

The boys seemed quite receptive to the idea. They had never been away from home by themselves before, but they were excited about receiving the video and finding out more. My daughter, on the other hand, would not even discuss it. She had absolutely no intention of going to that camp and there was no way in which I could make her. I knew I was in for a battle.

When the video arrived, the boys watched it and asked many questions. They were nervous but also excited. Emma wouldn't look at it. She had dug in her heels. Every opportunity she had she would tell me that she wasn't going. Nevertheless, I decided to sign up all three for the camp, and tell them that I thought they should go.

I went out and bought camp supplies for them and talked about what to expect. Emma silently fumed and refused to get involved. One night all her anger erupted. She yelled at me with all her fury and slammed the door in my face. She cried hysterically. She was shaking. She told me that she really didn't want to go and how could I make her. Couldn't she please stay home and I could just make the boys go? She insisted that she was fine and didn't need to go to this camp to "heal." She pleaded with me. She wanted only to be home with her friends. That was what she thought she needed most.

It was very difficult for me to force her to go, but as a parent I felt fairly confident that it was the right choice for her. I loved her and I had to show my love for her by making her do this for herself. However, it was scary for me. I knew that if she had a miserable time, I would never hear the end of it and that some of my credibility as a parent and what I thought was best for her would be destroyed. I had already made a mistake in sending her back to the soccer field too soon. I didn't want to traumatize her again with something so new and different.

In the end, I made a deal with her. I told her that if she really hated it, I would pick her up after three days, but she had to agree to give it three days. I also told all my children that I was going to go and stay at a hotel near the camp so that if they needed me, I would be there for them. Plus, I needed to be close to them for my own reasons. Being away from them for a week made me feel nervous and uncomfortable. I needed to feel that I could get to them if I wanted to.

Putting them on the bus as they departed up north to the Berkshires in western Massachusetts was very difficult for all of us. As the date drew near, the boys had grown scared and uncertain, as if the fact that they'd never been away from home before was finally sinking in. Now they were not only leaving home but also going away to a place where they would have to confront their grief. Though the camp had the no-pressure-to-talk-about-it atmosphere I'd been seeking, the fact remained that it was designed exclusively for children of 9/11 victims. If I had let them, all three would have jumped off that bus and right back into my car.

But I had made my decision and despite my own worry, ultimately I still felt that it was the right thing for all of them. It had been almost a year since David's death and, selfishly, part of me was now looking forward to having some time to myself. I thought this time away from my children would allow me to have that, and afterward, I could greet my children with renewed strength and resolve, able to focus back on their needs.

One night earlier, when I was talking with my daughter and encouraging her about the camp, I had told her that at worst, she could just sit around and do pottery for the week; at best, it would benefit her in many ways. It would be good for her to be with other peers who could understand her turmoil, and even if it didn't help now, maybe it would help her twenty years from now. At least she would be making that connection. Besides, even if it didn't help her and she was fine, maybe she would help somebody else, and that in itself would give her strength and help her to heal.

The camp sent digital photos of the children every day, and it was very reassuring for me to see their smiling faces. Of course, the first picture that I saw of Emma was her sitting at a potter's wheel. She was really going to kill me, but it did make me chuckle. Fortunately, she didn't stay at the wheel for long, and all three ended up having a wonderful week.

At the camp's farewell banquet, one boy and one girl were chosen to give a speech about their experience at camp. Emma was chosen to represent the girls, and when it came time for her to speak, she got up and told of her trepidation about coming to camp. She admitted how much she didn't want to go and how she just about hated her mother for forcing her. But after the week, Emma had come to accept that I had made the right choice for her. She told the campers and staff that her stay at camp had been one of the best experiences of her life. She was so thankful she had gone. Her mother had been right.

A large number of the counselors told me about the wonderful speech Emma had given, and after hearing about it, I felt vindicated and relieved. I was careful not to rub it in Emma's face but I did ask her about the speech and compliment her on the job she had done. I realized that as a parent, it is really up to me to decide what is best for my children. I need to love them, and the best way to do that is to sometimes make difficult choices for them. I won't always make the right decisions, but when I do, it will justify the importance of my role and help them to develop into better human beings. It would be important for me to be their mother but not always their friend.

When I arrived at camp to pick up the children, we were all thrilled to see one another. It had been a healthy break for all of us. The boys eagerly showed me their cabin and bunk area and gave me a tour of the facilities. Ian was particularly proud of one of his accomplishments and was desperate to share it with me. It turned out to be a ropes course set high in the trees. All of my children are terribly fearful of heights. To complete this course, Ian had to muster the courage to climb up a swinging ladder about twenty feet up a tree and then cross from one tree to the next on a narrow plank with only a thin rope for stability. Looking up, I was sure that this activity would not have been first on my list of fun things to do. But he did it, and he had every right to feel proud of himself. I was so happy for him. He was developing confidence in spite of his loss. He was feeling secure in his environment and reaching out for new and exciting challenges.

Matthew and Emma also seemed to make great strides in their paths toward healing. I could tell by their confidence as we wandered around the camp and connected with their counselors, and my children seemed to appreciate my genuine interest in where they'd spent the last week. I'd realized anew that it means a lot to children when you make an effort to see and understand their lives.

I also realized during this week apart, how important it was to let the children know I was constantly thinking of each of them. The camp had suggested that parents write a letter to their child every day. In order to do this, one had to begin writing and mailing the letters about four days before the child left for camp. I didn't want my children to know that I was writing to them because I wanted it to be a surprise, so every day I would hide myself away and write each one a letter telling them what was going on and what I was thinking. When I asked them if they had received my letters, they groaned yes. They said that I was the only mom they knew of who wrote a letter every day. They said it was embarrassing. I didn't care and frankly I don't think they minded either. I think it added a measure of comfort, especially in the early days given how apprehensive they were about leaving home.

Bedtime can be the hardest time for confronting grief, but in the solitude and stillness of nightfall, it is the easiest time to show your love. Take a deep breath and curl up with your child. Slow things down and let your mind clear. Bedtime was a particularly good time for me to figure out what was on the minds of my children. I would let long silences hang, giving my children time to sort out their thoughts while secure in my embrace. I would prompt them, hopeful that they might have the courage to discuss a memory or emotion. But even if they wouldn't speak, they would always listen. It seemed that listening to my thoughts helped them to clarify theirs.

Ian and Matthew wanted me to talk with them for ages at bedtime. Sometimes I didn't have much patience but I would always talk with them even briefly. I would tell them truthfully that I was tired or not feeling well and that I couldn't speak with them for long. Because I was consistent with my bedtime routine and honest with my feelings, they didn't object when I had time for only a brief conversation. They understood that I would talk to them for as long as I could. Five minutes of talking to and listening to your child is enough for a child to know that you love them.

I also knew that with or without our discussions, the quiet evenings, when thoughts seem to stir and memories come flashing back, could cause all sorts of emotions to bubble up. Because of this, you may find that your child might fear sleep. I know that mine did, which is why Ian wanted to sleep with the light on all night. I would let him keep it on until he fell asleep and then turn it off when I was going to bed, though occasionally Ian wanted it on all night.

In addition, both boys wanted frequently to sleep with me, and I would let them do that, too. I knew that Ian and

Matthew wanted to sleep in my bed for the security; and I knew that I could always move them into their own bed when I needed to go to sleep. Also, I limited the times that they were permitted in my bed. I didn't want it developing into a habit and I needed some time to be alone at night, too.

However you handle these kinds of typical requests and behaviors, just don't shun children or tell them everything is fine. Your children will get over their fear but it will take time. I had to be patient and I needed to accommodate their needs. It is the process of grief.

Every night now when I put my children to bed, I give them two kisses. I used to just give them one kiss, but since the death of their father, I've changed my routine. On one cheek, I kiss them and tell them good night and to sleep well. I also tell them that I love them. On the other cheek, I kiss them from their dad and tell them good night and to sleep well and that he loves them. They have taken so much comfort in this new routine that if I forget to kiss a cheek, they quickly remind me and make me redo the ritual. That combination of love and routine seems to go a long way. It makes them feel loved and it makes us all smile.

What You Can Do
to Guide Your Child with Love

- Say "I love you" as many times a day as you are able and show a child your love with your actions.
- Hug your child. Kiss your child. Listen to your child. And praise your child.

- At bedtime, give a child at least five or ten minutes of your undivided attention. Ignore the phone and other demands and focus on your child. Curl up and comfort your child.

- Let your child know that you are there for him, and be sincere in your words. When your child needs you, don't block out him or her or bury yourself in your own grief. Come to the rescue with a hug, an ear, or a gentle reassurance.

- Combine routine with love by developing a new evening ritual when putting your child to bed or saying good night. A back rub, a story, or reciting prayers can be very soothing.

- If a child upsets you with bad behavior, reprimand the behavior and not the child. Tell the child that the behavior is inappropriate and unacceptable. Let the child know that you love him but not his behavior.

- Give unconditional love, but set boundaries for your child's behavior.

- Loving a child means being a parent and helping a child through right and wrong. Don't use grief as an excuse for forgiving or allowing bad behavior.

- Be a parent, not a friend. Your child may have many friends but limited parents.

- Loss requires more patience and tougher decisions. Stick to your family values and combine love with expectation.

- Reward and praise small accomplishments. Take joy in your steps toward healing.

- Children need love in different ways. Some children may need comforting bedtime conversation, some may need to be held, and others might need constant attention and reassurance.

- Love can mean going against a child's wishes, such as sending your child to camp or involving your child in a support group or grief therapy. Do what is in your child's best interest. You are the parent. Offer a compromise if needed to give the child more of a sense of control in the decision.

- Don't be afraid of mistakes. With love comes risk.

- Don't be overprotective. Guarding your child from all the outside elements is doing that child a disservice. A child needs to heal, and healing involves pain.

- If you truly love a child, the child will love you in return.

- Grief causes insecurity. Loving a child will help that child to regain some security.

Honesty

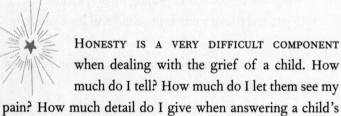

Honesty is a very difficult component when dealing with the grief of a child. How much do I tell? How much do I let them see my pain? How much detail do I give when answering a child's questions? Do I talk with them about things if they haven't brought them up?

When my husband died, the first difficult bit of truth came when I had to tell them that their father was missing and probably dead. They wanted to believe that he was okay and just missing. Maybe he hadn't had time to get in touch with us yet. I actually didn't have any specific knowledge that he was dead, but I saw the building that he was trapped in collapse and my senses knew he had perished along with it. He had called me from his office on the eighty-third floor to tell me that he loved the children and me, and that he couldn't get to the stairwell. He was trapped. Smoke was overcoming him and his lungs were burning. Shortly after we hung up, the building collapsed, so I didn't have much hope. How much of this reality should I share with my children?

To allay any doubt that he was in the building and that he had been trapped, I told my children that their father had called me and what his situation was. I also told them that he wanted them to know that he loved them very much.

I explained a little more. While trapped, he was working very hard to comfort his two female associates and trying to discover a solution to their horrible situation. I told them how brave he was and how clever he had been during the panic. I also told them that he was able to laugh while he spoke with me. If the children knew he could laugh, then maybe they wouldn't worry as much about his fears. I told them that they should be very proud of their father's bravery. And lastly, I let them know that he wasn't in any pain, and that when he did die, if in fact he had, his death would have been painless, as the smoke would have just put him to sleep.

I decided to tell them all that because it was the truth to the best of my knowledge, and I knew that those facts would help to comfort them. Whether David was killed by suffocation from the smoke, the collapse of the building, or something else didn't matter. We would never know the answer to the cause of his death so why should I further torment the children with other, more frightening possibilities? Honesty doesn't mean that one has to discuss everything. Just be honest with what you feel the child needs to know, thinking carefully about what those needs really should be.

Months later I was having a conversation with my children when the subject of bravery came up. Ian suddenly made a comment about what his dad would have done in the situation and that he doubted he would ever be as brave as his father was. This all stemmed from Ian's memory of my conversation with the children on that tragic day of David's death. Clearly, Emma, Ian, and Matthew had absorbed every word. Thank goodness I had not told them a lie that would come back to haunt me. I agreed with Ian that his dad was indeed very brave, but I also told him that his own bravery might surprise him one day. After all, hadn't he been very brave in dealing with his father's death? Ian thought about my question for a moment and then smiled and said, "I guess." I think my praise helped him to feel a little better about himself.

As time marched on following the tragedy and we didn't have a confirmation of David's death, it was difficult. I decided not to let them hear, read, or see any of the media coverage of the event because I could not see it serving any purpose and it would only add to their stress. Personally, I couldn't continue to see images of the falling towers flashed on the screen or hear reports from eyewitnesses on the radio. It was too overwhelming and painful. And as I didn't want my children's grief to become any more traumatized by the media, the television was turned to only one kid-friendly channel, the newspaper was immediately recycled, and the radio remained off.

My children seemed fine not hearing or reading anything more about the event. They relied on my judgment and honesty to tell them what they needed to know. My sons fully accepted my reports and accounts, and they never questioned my authority. But my daughter, being a little older, was more uncertain. As far as she was concerned, I had made mistakes before, so maybe I hadn't gotten the whole story quite right this time. Maybe I was mistaken. Maybe her father was alive.

I tried to read them books to help them deal with their grief, but my daughter resisted. One night she became very angry with me when I spoke of David in the past tense. Why was I always insisting he was dead when he might not be? For all we knew he was wandering around New York City confused from a bump on the head. Maybe he was in a hospital somewhere. I had called the hospitals to try to locate him, but I decided not to tell her that. For the moment, I decided that her denial and anger were part of her grieving process and I had to allow her that. So I apologized and told her she was right. Her father might actually still be alive and it was wrong of me to be so pessimistic. Then I gave her a very big hug and told her that I loved her. From then on, I carefully chose my words in front of her.

In every situation, honesty is a very personal judgment call. The grieving process is different for every child and his or her caregiver. But some honesty is very important, even if the honesty is nothing other than you don't know what to do or say. Just be sincere in your remarks, and sensitive to your child's age and maturity. You may not want to explain something to a four-year-old the same way as you would to a fourteen-year-old.

When you are talking with your child, he or she will soon perceive if you are telling him or her the truth or if you are avoiding something with lies, so if you don't want to tell a child something, let your child know. Tell her that you don't feel she needs to know at that moment and close the conversation. It can be addressed at a later date or when you know what to say.

Don't be afraid to admit to a mistake or that you have no idea what the future holds. It's all right to tell your children that you don't know what to do or that you don't have all the answers. It's all new territory for all of you. You're in this together. Your honesty will comfort them and your sincere communication will give a child more security.

A child, no matter the age or the personality of that child, should always be told the truth about certain things— such as a parent, grandparent, or sibling dying. How, what, or when you say it is up to you, but certain truths cannot be ignored. One truth or reality that I chose to shield my children from, however, was sorting through David's clothes. Not only did I not want to talk about it in front of the children, I also did not want them to see me doing it. It was going to be hard enough for me. I didn't need to stress them out, too. So when my kids were at school, I slowly began the process. Certain articles of clothing I kept in hopes that eventually Emma, Ian, or Matthew might want them. Some of my friends told me that they cherish articles of clothing from a late parent. Hopefully mine will, too, and when the time is right, I will let my children know what I have done.

Another very difficult time for me was when I was informed that they had identified my husband. I decided not to tell the children until the following afternoon. It was late Sunday night, six weeks after the tragedy and two days after my fortieth birthday, when the police came to my door. I didn't want to wake up the children with such traumatic news; nor did I want to tell them right before they went off in their mad rush to school the following morning. I decided that I would tell them after I had picked them up from school, and when I had them all together. So I waited.

It was a very difficult day. I was terrified. I remember working out at the gym, trying to calm myself down and formulate my words for when I would tell the children. I knew how the news affected me and how it had sent me back, and I was dreading Emma's, Ian's, and Matthew's reactions and added grief. On September 11, when I saw the horror unfold on television, my initial reaction was shock. Then as time went by, physical symptoms attacked my body. My throat began closing up. My eyelid started continually twitching. I was sweating profusely, particularly my hands and feet. Although exhausted, I couldn't get my mind to let in sleep. My breath became stale and I had a metallic taste in my mouth. I was continually thirsty. I had no appetite. Now, with the news that David had been found, these symptoms began to flood back. Would my children have to relive their distress as well? Had they felt some of these same symptoms? How could I put them through that?

When I picked them up from school, I felt ill. My stomach was in knots and I was shaking. This was a very difficult truth for me to tell. Finally, when we got home I turned off the car and told them to stay seated for a minute because I had something to tell them. I had spent all morning at the gym burning off my stress, trying to think of an appropriate way to tell my children the news, with many scenarios playing through my head, deciding that simplicity and direct honesty would be best. I didn't want to leave any room for doubt or miscommunication.

So I told them very directly: "Daddy's dead body has been found." That was it. That was all I said. I had thought all day about what words to use, and how much to tell them. I knew that I had to use the word "dead" so that they didn't think he was still alive. When I was finished, they looked at me and said okay. I was shocked at their reaction. No tears, no questions. If anything, there was relief. Then, they hopped out of the car, went into the house, and got themselves a snack.

I never anticipated it to transpire that way. But looking back on it, I realize that it gave them some closure. Later on, I told them that authorities had told me that his body had been found on the day the building collapsed, so he had definitely died right away. I also told them that his body was being sent to a funeral home nearby and that he was going to be cremated. I explained what cremation meant when they asked, telling them that their grandfather had also been cremated. Cremation was a form of burial, or a ritual, that some people choose for when they die; so Daddy's remains would be the same as many other people's. He would be no different.

After that, I realized that as children, Emma, Ian, and Matthew might respond differently to the truths that I told them. As an adult, I had more information and would analyze things differently. A truth I learned might have very different implications for me from the same truth told to my children and their processing of it, and I really had no idea how my kids would react. Just because I thought they might react terribly was no reason to withhold certain truths from them. Sometimes, it would be in their best interest for me to be honest with them and to give them information.

Each child is a different individual with a different personality and a different life experience. Each child may react differently to information. As a caregiver, don't try to anticipate a child's every reaction. It's impossible. Instead, think about who you are talking to, what you need to say, and how best to say it.

I am very glad that I told my children their father had been found. It was such a relief for me when it was over, especially when they seemed accepting. It was the right thing to do, although it was very difficult and frightening. I spent a lot of time thinking about the situation and trying to listen to my instincts. I also tried to take clues from my children. My daughter's fear that her father was walking around as a homeless person would always persist until she knew he had been found. Also, I didn't give them more information than they needed to know. If they had questions, I would answer them. If they didn't, I would leave it at that.

Children appreciate honesty. Let them see you cry. Let them know you are sad or scared or suffering from the loss of a loved one. Let them know that you don't have all the answers and are only trying your best.

Don't be afraid to ask them for advice on how you could make them feel better, or what you could do to lessen their pain. Often, the lead for honesty will come from them. In a quiet moment, they may reach out to you. Answer them truthfully, but in a way that is age appropriate and won't cause them any further stress. Many times by asking questions, they are looking for comfort. Keep in mind, that with honesty, age appropriateness is very important. Be sensitive to that.

In addition, don't rush it. Many times a child may want to think about things before they are ready to confront them. Matthew didn't communicate about his dad for a long time. Gently, slowly, and when we were alone, I would talk about how I was feeling. Sometimes I would just tell him a silly story about his father that I was reminded of that day. Often, I would simply tell Matthew how very much his father and I loved him. In time, he did reach out and start talking and asking. He had been feeling guilty about his dad's death and it took him a while to admit and talk about that. Then, it took him a while to get over his guilt and to move beyond it. My honesty, love, and bedtime routine with Matthew gave him security. That security permitted Matthew to be able to trust me, and in turn, allowed him to be honest with me.

David's birthday fell about eight months after his death. I debated for many weeks about what to do on this day. I knew that I didn't want us to just sit around. Somehow, I wanted to honor his memory, so I decided that his birthday would be the time for us to visit where he was killed, Ground Zero. I knew that enough time had elapsed, so that the site would be fairly cleaned up. None of us had been to the site since his death.

Furthermore, after we went to Ground Zero, I thought we could do something that David would have liked to do. So I made plans to go out to lunch and then to the American Museum of Natural History and the planetarium. I invited some of our good friends along to drive us into the City and to support us throughout the day.

I told my children well in advance about my idea. I thought that it would give them time to think about my itinerary and to come up with any questions or thoughts that they might have. They seemed to think that it sounded like a good idea, and that their father would have enjoyed revisiting the museum.

I didn't talk about Ground Zero much. I was nervous about going and I wasn't exactly sure what to expect from the site, the children, or myself, and I didn't want to focus on it too much until I had to. I decided my kids would ask me questions if they had any, but I didn't want to bring up things that might lead to questions that I didn't want to answer. Since David's death, I had kept Emma, Ian, and Matthew very protected from every vision or commentary concerning Ground Zero.

Then one day, as the date was approaching, Emma came home and remarked that she didn't know that her friend Katie was going with us to New York to celebrate her dad's birthday. She then asked me what Ground Zero was. I was so shocked she didn't know. My community, friends, and family had worked together so hard to protect my children. Had I forgotten how heavily I had shielded them? Here I was talking about Ground Zero and my children didn't even know what that meant. Why didn't they ask me? It was only after her friend talked about it that Emma wanted to know exactly what was going on.

After I explained to her what Ground Zero was, I quickly went upstairs and told her brothers. They all processed the information without incident and still thought our itinerary for the day was fine. I guess they had no better idea about what to do on their father's birthday, so they were leaving it up to me. They trusted my judgment.

When the day finally arrived, I was quite anxious. Once we arrived at Ground Zero, the ride up in the elevator to the private family viewing room was no easier. Sometimes anticipation is worse than facing your fears. The children had been acting out all morning, being fresh and hyper, particularly Emma and Matthew. I had no idea why they were being so difficult. Actually, I didn't give it much thought because I was so stressed. I just found it to be annoying.

Once we entered the viewing room, my children seemed to calm down and feel at ease. They looked at the footprints of the Twin Towers, watching the trucks clearing the site. We were up very high, enclosed in a large room with a wall of glass overlooking the footprints, so our proximity to the site felt a bit less threatening. My kids walked around the room absorbing all of the personal, tragic information on the walls, and they each wrote a note to David in the guest book wishing him a happy birthday. When we finally left, they were looking forward to the rest of the day.

That night, I lay in bed wondering what had made them so ornery. Thinking about it, I decided that they were really anxious, too. For all I knew, they were anticipating dead bodies and other gruesome scenes. Their information about the site was only that thousands of people had died there. I'm sure they were worried about what exactly it would look like. By my giving them no information, I had let their minds wander and develop fantastic scenarios. I felt so bad that I had put them through that unnecessary stress. I don't think that my children had discussed it with me beforehand because, as I felt, it was easier to ignore. When the day finally arrived and they were faced with the reality, they started freaking out.

I realize that I should have not made any assumptions. How could they possibly have known that the site had been cleared when they didn't even know what Ground Zero was? I should have given them some honest information to protect them. The grieving process is a learning process for both caregiver and child.

Another difficult aspect of honesty can be with practical matters. I had to draw up a new will after my husband died. The children didn't need to know that, but I did want to talk with them about their guardians in the event that I should die. Now, I had some thought that bringing up this subject would cause my children additional, new stress. But I felt that if I was thinking about this, surely they must be, too. After all, were they not calling me from school to check that I was all right? Were they not terrified every time I became sick or injured? They had given me the clues, and they deserved my honesty.

So one night at the kitchen table I told them that I was trying to decide who should become their guardians in the event of my death. I quickly let them know that I had no intention of dying and that everything was fine, but that I wanted to be prepared just in case something unforeseen happened. I wanted to make sure that they were comfortable with what would happen to them.

I had thought about my choices and rather than give them carte blanche, I told them that they had a choice between guardians "a" or "b." I listed the pros and cons of both and answered any questions they had. Of course, I had spoken with both couples beforehand to make sure they were willing to be guardians, and I told these people that I was going to discuss it with the children before we made our decision.

My children were fine with the discussion. They listened attentively to my comments and I told them what I thought they wanted. Fortunately, they agreed with me. They were very happy that I had discussed it with them, and I think it reassured them that I was thinking and planning in a responsible and parentlike manner. I wasn't losing my marbles. I was still looking after them. I was being their mom.

I'm sure that you appreciate that all parents and children have a different relationship with each other; and many communicate in different ways and in different settings. But it is the communication and the honesty of the communication that is so vital to a child and his or her security. Don't think that you can easily fool a child, either. Children are very perceptive and pick up on things we think they may not understand. Never underestimate a child's intelligence.

In her early teens a friend of mine lost her mother. Quite shortly after her mother died, her father began a relationship with another woman. Her father told her that this woman was just his friend and meant nothing special. But my friend knew that her father and this woman were more than friends and she resented her father for the dishonesty. It still bothers her almost thirty years later. Her advice to me when David died was to be honest with my children about important issues that would directly affect them. Children will figure it out for themselves anyway, so tell them the truth. Don't be afraid, although it may be hard, and be willing to have an honest discussion with your child. Perhaps through talking, issues may be resolved or fears may be addressed that would otherwise lay dormant and fester.

One thing that was on my mind and caused me stress

when it came to honesty was the concept of remarriage and dating. Being a single parent is a bit overwhelming, even in the best of circumstances, and I knew that I really didn't want to stay single for the rest of my life. I was only thirty-nine when David was killed, and the thought of perhaps another forty years alone was very depressing. I had loved being married and being a family and we were all craving the lost companionship of a father and husband. I also felt that remarriage would benefit the children (providing I made a suitable choice). Although not a biological parent, a stepparent can be a wonderful support and role model for a child, and getting back a father figure and sharing the responsibilities of parenthood can strengthen a family environment.

Personally, one of the hardest things for me about losing David was the loneliness. I wondered if the children yearned for him as I did. For over a year after his death, I would wake up in the morning and expect him to be lying in bed next to me. What a rude awakening when reality set in. I didn't like the feeling. So although I hoped to remarry, I knew I had to come to terms with being alone, just as my children had to come to terms with not having a father. It would be a challenge for all of us to learn to love life again without sharing our lives with David. We had to readjust. We had to learn to be content with taking pleasure from life itself and our new family.

However, dating and remarriage were on my mind, and another facet of those thoughts was guilt. I loved David very much and the concept of loving another man made me feel disloyal. Furthermore, I worried that the children would also view my dating as disloyal. I worried about Emma's, Ian's, and Matthew's perceptions of marriage. I didn't want them to think that it was easy to jump from one spouse to another, and that I didn't still love their father. My daughter was thirteen; setting a responsible precedent was equally important. I had to be very careful how I behaved myself. When I was ready, casual dating had to be away from the house allowing no interaction with the children. Frankly, I didn't even want my children to know when I was going on a date. That makes honesty and dating a very tricky combination. In addition, I didn't want them to think that just because I was dating someone, it meant he would be their future stepfather and that he would replace David.

I decided to once again listen to my instincts. If I began to care about someone, I would not rush into anything, but I would take my time and make sure I wanted to develop a relationship with this person. For safety reasons, I would have to be careful not to give out my address. My first consideration was the safety of my children, both physically and mentally. Aside from the obvious perils, there is always the danger that by introducing someone to the children, Emma, Ian, and Matthew could become emotionally attached to that person. If he and I then broke up, losing another father figure could be traumatic for them.

But I did hope to eventually remarry and I wanted to be honest with them about my feelings. I was sure, too, that at least Emma had thought about the possibility of a new stepfather. Slowly, after it had been quite a while since David's death and when the opportunity arose, I began to mention re-marriage to the children. We never discussed it for long, but I wanted to know what they were feeling and what their thoughts were on the idea. I knew that Ian and Matthew's ini-tial reaction when I spoke with them that first night, of want-ing me to remarry immediately, was not in their minds now. Since then, they had told me that they didn't ever want me to remarry. Emma had remained silent on the subject. But now enough time had elapsed and they had calmed down, so I thought that if I started discussing it before I was actually in the situation of dating, it would be less threatening.

Initially, all three vehemently opposed the idea and ended the discussion. Ian went as far as to say that he was certain that I didn't want to ever get remarried. Of course, I had never said anything of the sort, but clearly that was what he wanted from me. But over time, they became more ques-tioning and open to the idea. I didn't bring it up often, but as time moved on and I became more ready to think about see-ing someone else, I pressed further.

One night over the dinner table, I was discussing re-marriage and asking each child individually what each felt. Both my boys said that they were getting used to the idea and that if he was nice and he didn't bring any other chil-dren into the mix, they might be okay with it. Emma told me that she would probably hate the man initially because that's how children are supposed to react to a stepfather. She said it was only normal. Over time, however, she thought that she could learn to like him. She just didn't want me to expect her to feel overjoyed and welcoming from the beginning. It

was going to be a slow process. Was the introduction of another man into our lives the right thing to do? Would it benefit my kids? I had to be careful and take my time. Just as
grief can be selfish, so can the desire to avoid loneliness. I
had to make sure that while my children were still under my
care, I chose remarriage only if it helped and strengthened
all of us.

About fifteen months after David's death, I started developing feelings for another man. I had been speaking with
him on the phone for a few months and we had become
friends. We had seen each other a couple times, but it was
platonic and I wasn't sure which way it was headed. I was
very careful not to speak with him around the children, but
somehow Ian was picking up something. One day, Ian told
me that he thought I had a boyfriend. I was shocked and immediately felt very embarrassed. I denied the accusation because I wasn't sure what else to say, and I was so taken off
guard. This man had never shown anything but friendship
toward me, but Ian still suspected something. After all, I was
speaking and spending time with a man whom they didn't
know and who hadn't been around before the death of their
father. Of all three of my children, Ian is the most protective
of me, perhaps because he sees himself as the oldest male
now that his father is deceased, and he is very keenly aware
of my actions.

It was hard for me to decide what to say to the children.
My friend's warning about her father and his hidden ro-
mance rang in my head, but so did a million other bells.
Friends kept on warning me about bringing a male into the

children's lives. They thought that until it was really serious, I shouldn't involve my children. My friends wanted to protect my children from any more pain. I was well aware of the risks to them and to me, but I wasn't entirely comfortable with my dishonesty, either. If I told them, maybe they would trust me more with the truth. But if I didn't and I went off for the day or evening, how well could I lie to them and how comfortable was I with my deception? If they found out I had lied to them, would they believe me in the future or always be suspicious of my personal life? As I continually tell my children, trust once broken is not an easy thing to fix.

Certainly, it was valid for me to tell my children that I was getting together with friends when I was going out, but my daughter was relentless in finding out all the details. She wanted to know what I was doing, with whom, when, and where. She didn't want me keeping anything from her. She wanted to know what was happening in my life.

After much thought, I decided to have another chat with them. Over dinner, I told them that I did in fact like someone, but I wasn't sure of his feelings for me. The questions came pouring out, but so did the support. Ian had a huge grin on his face and told me that he knew it. They then proceeded to ask me his name, what exactly was happening, and if I would see him again. I told them that we were just friends and that was all we might ever be, but that I did like him and I hoped that we would see each other again. I did tell them, though, that just because I liked someone, it didn't mean he was going to be their stepfather or even that we'd start dating. Things might not develop, but even if they did, I might not want to marry the man. I needed to get to know him better.

It was such a relief for me to be honest with my children. My relationship with this man was not serious, as we were just good friends, so it wasn't hard to discuss. Now whichever way the relationship turned, I could bring my children along to the next step. It would be a while, however, before this man was involved with their lives, if in fact he ever was. That I knew I had to be careful on. But for the present, they felt secure with my situation because of my honesty. They trusted my judgment.

As it turned out, nothing other than a good friendship developed in the relationship, but it taught me a great deal. I know I made the right choices. I learned that I could spend time with another man and not feel guilty, and my children learned to be comfortable with my honesty and choices when it came to dating. I am thankful that it was such a slow and careful process. For the moment, both the children and I are much more relaxed about the idea of a stepfather. They don't worry about me dating and don't think about it. The angst has dissipated, and my fears about dating in relation to my children have calmed. I am also so busy with our lives that I don't really have the time or energy to date. I am enjoying my children and cherishing our moments together. We are becoming a happy family again.

The more secure a child feels in a family, the less stress he or she will feel in the grieving process. Grief brings forth much insecurity. It is all about the unknown and its uncertainties. By combating those insecure feelings with love, routine, honesty, and security, a caregiver is giving a child the strength and the power to deal with the grief. You are helping the child to heal.

WHAT YOU CAN DO
TO GUIDE YOUR CHILD WITH HONESTY

- Honesty is difficult.
- The amount of truth divulged depends on the age, personality, and maturity of a child.
- Tell a child only what the child needs to know.
- Take your cues from a child. Listen to your child's thoughts and concerns and determine your child's needs. If a child is suffering from denial and anger, honest discussion of death and forgiveness may not be a constructive approach until a later time.
- Don't tell your child things that could cause further trauma or stress.
- Protect your child with your honesty. Children often ask questions for comfort and reassurance. Your honesty should try to calm fears rather than create them.
- Honesty is about needs—a child's needs, not your own. Be careful when figuring out those needs.
- The honesty of not knowing is okay; don't be afraid to tell a child you don't know.
- If the loss of a loved one involves media attention, do your best to protect your child from witnessing those

accounts. The truth is best handled traveling from you to your child. Not all media reporting is accurate, and your child may not be able to handle all of the information. Visions and reports could cause considerable additional distress.

- Reading to your child can lead to honest discussion regarding death.

- Respect your child's position in the grieving process. Don't belittle a child's feelings with disapproval.

- Use judgment in your honesty and don't force your child to hear something that the child isn't ready to handle.

- Some situations require absolute honesty. Telling a child of a loss or explaining changes in the child's life necessitates conversation.

- Certain truths can be avoided, such as those faced when sorting through the personal effects of the deceased.

- Choose an appropriate time to be honest. Don't deliver devastating news as you drop your child at school. Find a quiet and secure time when you can give your child your full attention.

- Don't assume a child's reaction to honesty. Children may react differently from one another and the caregiver.

- Be sensitive.

- Discussing issues before they become reality, such as dating or birthdays, can help ease tension and give better insight into everyone's feelings.

- Try not to deceive a child. Children are very perceptive.
- Communicate with your feelings, and be patient. Allow honesty to come from within yourself. A child will take your lead and follow.
- Trust once broken is difficult to repair.

Security

I ALWAYS WANTED TO BE A MOTHER, BUT I DIDN'T want to be just a "regular" mother; I wanted to be a *great* mother. My children have always been paramount in my life, and my goal has been to raise them as responsible, caring, honest, and secure individuals. I take great pride in all their accomplishments, just as I feel tremendous anguish from their failures and sufferings. So, to see them grieve is beyond heartbreaking.

I felt I was well on the way toward raising my children into well-adjusted adults, with few insecurities and problems. But the sudden death of their father caused a real backward spiral in my goal as a mother.

All David and I had worked toward as parents suddenly seemed insignificant to what my children would have to endure and to what I would have to help them overcome. I really resented the thought that living with David's tragic death had ruined all my hard work as a mother, that all my accomplishments were futile and no longer mattered because my children's lives had become irreparably and uncontrollably altered. I was so angry that my dream for my children of stability and happiness would now never become reality. In the immediate aftermath of their father's death, I thought they would never be well-adjusted, secure adults.

As time goes by and as we are healing, my perception of Emma's, Ian's, and Matthew's development has changed, though my parenting skills are being put to the ultimate test. The fact is that because David and I were able to give our children a secure base on which to start their lives, I believe they are having a bit of an easier time dealing with their grief. My parenting is still the same parenting. My children know they are loved, they know there is honesty in our relationship, and they have routine; as a result, they also feel a sense of security. I now realize that it is precisely *because* of my efforts that my children will endure. Routine, love, honesty, and security—what children need when they grieve— are what I have *always* given my children, but now my philosophies are being strengthened and reinforced.

So, it is your routine, your love, and your honesty that bring about security in a child's life. All this will help to lessen a child's fears and help a child pass through the grieving process. Just remember to always be a parent. Don't try to be a friend. Don't become an enemy. Just be a parent, someone who loves and protects them, and someone who makes them feel secure.

One night over dinner, close to a year and a half after David's death, Ian, Emma, and I were talking. Somehow the subject of 9/11 came up and I asked them if the subject was still discussed at school. Ian said that some of the teachers had brought it up when a discussion in class turned to world events or some other such topic connected to a tragedy. Curious, I asked how he felt about that. He said that he didn't mind when the teacher mentioned it, but the reaction of his classmates, as every head in the classroom simultaneously turned toward him, was uncomfortable. He demonstrated the motion to me, and his reenactment really made me laugh. But demonstrations aside, what did Ian do? He said that he just ignored everyone and pretended that nothing strange was happening. Emma said that the same thing happens to her and that she, too, just ignores it.

I told my children that they might always have things like that happen to them during the course of their lives, and that they may forever be known as 9/11 children. They responded by saying that they had thought about that, too. And they were okay with knowing that that could certainly be the truth. This life had become their new normal and they would adjust and cope. It was fine. I felt so proud of them because they had revealed to me that they were gaining security with whom they had become.

My children have made great strides in their journey of grief. They continue to heal and to grow stronger. Our community, friends, and family have helped us, and this support has enabled me to be a better parent and my children to reach out.

Interestingly enough, since David's death, my children told me that they have never spoken alone with each other about their father and their feelings. They speak with each other when I am around or they mention something in passing to each other, but they have never reached out to one another for support, at least in a traditional sense. Other than knowing they have one another and that they are together in this situation, Emma, Ian, and Matthew treat one another no differently. Whether an only child would have a more difficult time with the loss of a parent would seem to depend on the personality of that child. Some children probably would reach out to a sibling, but mine chose not to. Emma found her friends to be more of a support for her and she would discuss things with them before her brothers, whereas her brothers turned only to me as their sounding board.

Although I am still their primary support, my children are opening up to others more frequently. As time passes, they feel more secure because their trust in our new environment has strengthened through my consistent display of love, routine, and honesty. With the added security, my children feel better about themselves and more readily acknowledge and share their accomplishments. You may discover as I did, that after the death of a loved one, at times, your child may become dispirited and overwhelmed with sadness. This sadness can make it difficult for a child to feel positive toward him- or herself. But by guiding a child to accept a loss with routine, love, and honesty, you will help your child's self-esteem to strengthen; and with that growing sense of security, your child will be more willing to stand alone with confidence and pride.

David's family wanted to honor David's memory with a memorial soccer trophy. It is a stunning silver cup awarded each autumn to a young female soccer player who demonstrates David's values of loyalty, team spirit, ability, and support both on and off the soccer field. The first season, it was awarded to David's entire team; but the second season Emma was the sole recipient—Emma, who nearly gave up soccer altogether. She was so pleased. With the entire student body in attendance, the school held a ceremony to present Emma with the cup. It was a very special moment. Emma and her brothers all agreed that they would stand up by the podium in support of one another as the principal remembered David and recognized Emma. In a united display, and for the first time since their father's memorial service, my children willingly demonstrated their confidence and strength with smiles and grace. They had the security to challenge their own vulnerability, and with tears blurring my vision, I felt very proud.

After that things got easier, and Ian and Matthew had their turn in the spotlight as well. Both boys were two out of ten children chosen to represent their school, each boy on one of the two school teams, in a "brain bowl" competition. It was a state program for the gifted and talented in which schools would compete against one another for the championship "brain bowl" title. The questions in the event were all-encompassing and consisted of everything from trivia to science to current events.

The competition began with timed, preliminary rounds; the top two teams moved on to the final, buzzer round. I helped out as a moderator and found many of the questions to be beyond my capacity. It was so thrilling when the final results came in for the championship match. Both the boys' teams had won and were going to compete against each other in the final round. Seeing Ian and Matthew together on stage that evening filled me with joy. What a special moment and how proud their father would have been of them. Although nervous, my sons were happy, confident, and enjoying every minute of the spotlight, and they appeared no different from their teammates; no one in the audience, including myself, could see their grief.

Let your child know how proud you are of him or her. Let your child know that you know how difficult the grieving process is and what a terrific job you think he or she is doing handling it. With grief, children need to learn to feel good about themselves. Allow your child the security to feel good by, in part, taking pride in their accomplishments, however small or insignificant. Learn to celebrate life.

One thing death brought home to me was the brevity of life. Rather than waste my time continually anguishing over David's death, I wanted to enjoy what I had. I wanted to enjoy my children. Although you may not immediately have the strength to do so, in time, try to enjoy your child. Capture all that is wonderful about your child and celebrate. And try to be a positive role model for your child. By staying positive, when you are able, you are making your child feel more secure because you are showing your child that you, too, can be strong and heal.

Another way to help your child gain strength and feel more secure is to reward your child and yourself for victories over grief. Sometimes, when any one of my kids would do a little something to make any of us smile—like draw a funny picture or play a great game of soccer—I would take them all out for ice cream. Don't just try to cheer them up when they seem down. Celebrate and praise them for who they are. Lighten the road to healing with joy.

In the beginning, finding joy for a child or an adult suffering loss may be difficult to do, particularly with the burden of guilt. I don't recall the first time my children smiled after David's death, but I remember the first time my daughter really seemed happy and I smiled without feeling guilty. It was Emma's thirteenth birthday party. Emma's birthday came three weeks after David's death. Her friends wanted to try to cheer her up and to make her birthday special. It was her entrance into teenhood. With the help of their mothers, the girls organized a surprise party for Emma. When the day came, she wasn't particularly surprised but she was happy. It was the first time I had seen her celebrate, running around surrounded by peers and beaming with pleasure. Suddenly, I realized that I was smiling without guilt. Seeing her so happy helped me to find unburdened joy.

Knowing what to say and when to say it, if at all, is not an easy decision. As a caregiver, you and you alone must ultimately decide what is best for your child. Other people can help; but it is your knowledge of and relationship with your child that are the final decisive tools. Be a parent. Don't make your child your confidant or your crutch. Be there for them and love them. Although painful, the healing process will bind you closer together and you will help each other to heal.

However difficult it seems, don't give up. Your child needs you. Regardless of the type of loss a child has endured, security from a caregiver is paramount to healing.

By giving your child routine, love, and honesty, you are giving that child security. Security comes from you, the caregiver, and how you choose to respond to and with your child. If you are able to give your child security, your child has the power to develop the confidence he or she needs to become a responsible adult. Your child has the power to return the strength you have given him or her. Eventually, your child will be able to give his or her own child that same security and love. Your child will have the strength to see the good out of the bad, and he or she will endure and rise above the grief. Your child will heal.

WHAT YOU CAN DO
TO GUIDE YOUR CHILD WITH SECURITY

- Security helps a child to heal.
- Routine, love, and honesty all lead to security.
- Good parenting helps when navigating through the murky waters of grief.

- Parenting during grief is still parenting. The challenge is only greater. Principles should stay resolute.
- Love and protect your child without judgment.
- The way you choose to lead your life will be witnessed and absorbed by your child. Your insecurity or your stability will be reflected in your child.
- Encourage your child to face fears and to challenge vulnerability. Support your child in all the child's efforts. Your child will gain strength through his or her accomplishments and become more secure with the new strides toward victory.
- Enjoy your child's special moments. Let a child know how proud you are and how proud the lost loved one would be.
- Celebrate life.
- Lighten the road to healing with joy. Organize a surprise party, whisk away a child to a favorite restaurant or spend a day at the beach.
- A child needs a caregiver for support, guidance, and protection. Be there.
- Empower your child with routine, love, honesty, and security: These are the tools that will help a child to gain strength and to rise above grief.

PART FOUR

HOW OTHERS CAN HELP

Setting Up a Network

PROVIDING ASSISTANCE TO A GRIEVING FAMILY can be an invaluable gift. Allowing a caregiver to focus more attention on a child will help a grieving child tremendously. But how or when to help is a very difficult and tricky question. Finding the right balance between assistance and invasion or privacy and loneliness is challenging. Even the grief-stricken family won't always know the answer. But one thing is certain: Someone other than the grieving family needs to attempt to set up a network.

On September 11, as events unfurled before my eyes, a form of paralysis overtook my body. I could hear. I could see. I could walk. I could do all the necessary motions. But what I couldn't do was think clearly or process information.

My mind buried itself within a protective shell, allowing no information in or out. I was like a robot, making the movements but not feeling or thinking anything. I just sat dazed in my living room, not knowing what to do, staring at my fireplace. I felt so totally overwhelmed. I didn't know where to begin other than by protecting my children.

Time seemed to be in a dimension all its own. Hours seemed to go by unaccounted for and stand still at the same time. It's like an accident when everything seems to transpire in slow motion, and when the danger has passed, what had felt like five minutes had actually been only five seconds. That was my continual perception of time during my early stages of grief: fleeting and yet stationary. Consequently, I had little awareness of when it was time for me to feed my children or put them to bed. Emma, Ian, and Matthew were in their own fog anyway so they weren't exactly time conscious either. During those first few days, it took every ounce of energy I had to perform my most basic functions such as control my breath, stay warm, and calm my body down from its continual shaking. It was very difficult for me to focus on my children. Giving them the love, reassurance, and attention that they needed was about all I could achieve beyond my own existence—and it was hard to give them even that.

Thankfully, I had friends or family with me at every moment to help my children and me cope. My brother managed to get out of New York City that morning. He jumped on a train to Connecticut, rented the last car available, picked up my sister, and headed to my home in New Jersey. By evening, my two siblings had arrived and my friends were able to return to their own families. My brother and sister remained with me until my parents arrived the next day.

As nothing was moving in or out of my brain, it is impossible for me to recollect all of the details of those first days. But I do remember that the children and I had a friend or member of my family with us at all times for that first week or so. My sister even spent the night of September 11 in my bed with me, while my sons moved into a bedroom closer to me. Although my children seemed to eventually settle, neither my sister nor I got any sleep, but it was so reassuring to have someone next to me and to give me strength. I also think it made the children feel better knowing there was someone else in the house to take care of us.

As one can imagine, the phone never stopped ringing. If I had been alone, I'm sure that I would have just ignored it, which wouldn't have been the best thing given my children's need for a reliable mom and other people's need for information. My friends and family were concerned that the children and I were all right, and they wanted to find out what they could do to help. Having someone around to answer our phone and to direct assistance was a huge help to us.

The initial, most important thing that friends and family can do to help is to set up a network. Put one trusted person in charge and delegate. Perhaps that individual could be the first one to get in touch with the family or the first one to come stay with the family, but someone should take over to assist in running the household, especially when children are involved.

Once a person has stepped forward to be in charge of a support network, other helpers can follow. The support person can do only so much, so others can offer to take control of various tasks. I had different friends in charge of everything from organizing meals to babysitting. Think of it as a family tree, with one person at the top and all others branching down and forming other sectors of support, but all ultimately reporting back to the top. The person in charge can change as events, situations, or days evolve, but someone other than the grief-stricken individuals should always have the lead until slowly the family settles.

The leader of this network doesn't have to be staying with the family, although initially, it is infinitely easier. A concerned friend living far away would not know whom to phone and would inevitably call the grieving household to offer condolences or support. I didn't have the strength to answer my phone, and I certainly didn't want Emma, Ian, or Matthew to have to answer it. It took me about one month before I developed the courage to answer my phone, whereas the children didn't mind picking it up sooner. They wouldn't readily chat to whoever was on the other end, but Emma would answer in hopes it was one of her friends. Before then, if no one was available to answer a phone call for us, I would just let the answering machine pick up, although Emma was not keen to miss an opportunity for an invitation from a friend. Initially, however, having someone else responsible for answering the phone, returning the call when necessary, or taking a message was a tremendous relief to both my children and myself.

In the event it isn't feasible for the support person to stay with a grieving family, try to make sure that someone offers to collect messages and to return phone calls. If possible, try to have someone available to remain with the grieving family at least during the day. Deliveries of condolences, food, or flowers are most likely to occur and answering the door was not something the children and I were up to doing for at least a few weeks.

Even if a family wants to be alone, a support person could spend his or her time in a separate part of the house, allowing the family to maintain their privacy without interference. Most of my friends and family stayed out of our way while I hid in my living room or upstairs with my children. We never even came down to see friends who stopped by to offer their respects. It was all too hectic and emotional.

Sometimes phone calls, deliveries, and well-wishers can become exhausting for the support person, too. Try to find others willing to step in and help out from time to time. If there are any issues or questions over how things should be handled, everyone should know to contact the support leader rather than disturb the family.

One problem that my friends and family had to deal with was flowers. Huge arrangements were being delivered simultaneously from different florists. I didn't have enough space in my home to place them without rearranging my furniture, and Emma, Ian, and Matthew found the flowers disturbing. My friends decided to call the neighboring florists to ask them not to deliver flowers all at the same time, but to spread out the deliveries so we wouldn't feel so over-whelmed.

If you are a concerned friend or family member, think about when you choose to send flowers. Rather than sending them immediately upon hearing the news of a death or on the date of the funeral or memorial, consider a week or two later. Personally, like my children, I wasn't crazy about getting flowers. Ordinarily, I adore flowers, but receiving them for my husband's death was hard. To me, flowers are unique and beautiful, and I can't help but delight in their presence. To look at those arrangements and feel nothing but pain and despair spoiled the flowers for me. Although beautiful, they didn't cheer up the children or me.

I explained to my kids that flowers are sent to show sympathy and support, and I recognized and appreciated the gesture. Before the deliveries of the flowers, I had no idea any of us would react the way we did. It wasn't until the flowers arrived that our feelings arose. I distinctly remember the first arrangement being brought into our home and my own feelings upon seeing them. My thoughts were "The recognition of grief has begun. How utterly terrible." The reality of David's death was splendidly displayed before me, and the pain took my breath away. I felt a terrible pit in my stomach. The flowers represented my husband's absence so it was very hard to take any pleasure in their beauty. My children didn't clarify their feelings but they didn't show enthusiasm, either. They would have rather not had the flowers. I think they would have preferred "kid-friendly" food or computer games.

Not all grieving families may react to flowers as we did. Because there was so much uncertainty with David's death, flowers of sympathy were more difficult for us to accept than they might be for other families. We hadn't fully absorbed the reality of his death. In a different circumstance with a different family, flowers might well have been a comforting support. If you are reading this as a close friend or relative of a grieving family, knowing what is right to do is very difficult, but not doing anything can be worse.

Certain friends may want to initiate their own gesture of support. They should just inform a support person about their idea and then alleviate that person's burden by taking charge of the project on their own.

Although this book is about what *children* need when they grieve, a parent or primary caregiver also needs help during grief if he or she is to effectively guide a child through grief. The amount of support necessary to a caregiver can be estimated by the extent of the loss as it directly relates to the caregiver. If a child has lost a classmate, a caregiver's need for additional support would not be as great as in my instance, when I lost my husband. Also, given varying personalities of both guardian and child, or the number of children a guardian has to take care of, more or less support may be needed.

Recognizing that I needed strength in order to find strength for my children, some friends of mine wanted to do something really special for me. Knowing David's and my love of gardening, my friends wanted to ask the town to remember David with plants. On a set date, with a window of time, they asked the members of the community to drop off a yellow or white chrysanthemum plant at the bottom of my driveway. The colors represented hope and love, for our family. My friends called my home to make sure that the idea was okay with the kids and me. They also wanted to make sure that we were aware of the day and time it would take place. Strangely enough, although the children and I disliked receiving flowers, we agreed to their touching memorial, and on a cold and very rainy morning we were blessed and astonished to see car after car stop and place a potted chrysanthemum by our driveway. My two friends who had organized the event were waiting on my drive and decked out in full rain gear, taking and placing the plants side by side along the front wall of our property. By the time it was over, we had accumulated more than 150 beautiful plants. It was a wonderful show of support from the town, and my children and I were tremendously touched. Since the plants weren't placed in our home, the gesture wasn't as invasive as receiving flower arrangements, and the children didn't seem to mind. Quite dramatically, it demonstrated anew how much everyone cared and it gave us all strength.

As the days went on, and our flowers began to wilt from dryness, the local garden club was organized to water our thirsty gifts. Then, in time, the garden club gathered on our property and planted them. My friends had called my kids and me to make sure that we would want all this done. I said it would be fine provided I wasn't disturbed and it could be done while the children were at school. However much Emma, Ian, and Matthew appreciated the plants, they were still sensitive to having too much attention directed toward them. The garden club also wanted to know where we wanted the plants placed. Gardening was therapeutic for me, so rather than have the garden club decide where to dig, I decided that I wanted to figure it out for myself with input from the children if they so desired. Strolling around my yard, plants in hand, and analyzing plant placement was a pleasurable experience for me. It helped me to relieve stress and thus to accommodate my children's needs with just a little more patience. When the day came to plant, I even had the strength to briefly go outside and say hello and thank you to everyone. Although I didn't have the strength to dig, I enjoyed watching the process and, again, it soothed and regenerated my spirit. The garden looked spectacular when completed, but there were too many plants for even our large property to accommodate. The plants that we couldn't place in our garden, the children and I decided to give away to communal areas such as the local schools. For my family, it was healing to show our appreciation by making another environment a little bit brighter as well.

Other means of support to our family were suggested and executed during the beginning weeks of our grief. I am grateful that my friends and family members were able to set up an effective communication network. I know from experience that communication during the initial stages of grief must be ongoing and thorough. Mixed messages can be a waste of time and effort, and could possibly cause further stress to a grieving family. If, for example, the support person had spoken with the family and knew certain times visitors were welcome, but someone else misunderstood the request and told people that visitors should stay away, the grieving family could become distressed about people's reasons for avoiding them, and children might fear that their friends had rejected them. Additionally, if a grieving family needed the support or distraction of visitors but wasn't getting it, the emotional impact on the family could be significant.

It is very important for the individual building the network, or support person, to respect the choices of the grieving family. Although at times when trying to help a grieving family you may want to disagree with certain choices the family makes, individuals outside of the bereaved family must not proceed against the family's wishes. Grief is like a journey on which travelers may choose different paths. Certain decisions by a caregiver or a child might be made that in hindsight are considered mistakes, but such decisions are necessary journeys for some people and must be supported by friends and family. Although as an outsider to a family's individual grief you may not comprehend why a grieving family rejects offers of assistance, you must accept that family's choice. Just as a parent or guardian will sometimes get frustrated or disillusioned with a child's decision during times of grief, so, too, will a support person. In our case, I had a hard time accepting my daughter's denial of her father's death and her decision to reject me as insensitive. In time, she came to accept her dad's death and to welcome me back into her life, but she had to work through it in her own way, and although it wasn't my way, I had to understand and acknowledge it was hers.

Of course, if you are a friend wanting to give support and you observe any sort of danger to the welfare of a child, such as severe physical abuse or abandonment, certain measures must be taken even if the grieving family insists otherwise. Contacting a religious official or professional counselor to intervene and assess the situation would be advisable.

A parent's primary responsibility when a child is grieving is to help that child heal, and worrying about the wants and desires of a support person is rarely possible. When a family is grieving, politics and pleasantries may not be given much thought, and a caregiver will have little time to focus on anyone other than the child. A support person must understand this and not resent the family's actions. It is a very emotional time.

As a friend of mine told me, grief is like the ocean. One day it may be calm, but the next it may be full of waves. Let the family ride their waves regardless of how tumultuous they may be. Fighting the ocean is a losing battle.

The grieving family may choose to control certain responsibilities themselves. As a friend or family member, it is important to respect that choice. Don't undermine the family by taking care of something that perhaps a grieving child has voiced a desire to oversee. In a time of crisis, control may be something a child needs to help him through his grief. Just as my son Ian tried to regain a bit of control in his life by refusing to eat his dinner, a grieving child may want to take charge of something a support person might wish to do.

In every instance, whether my children or I wanted any involvement or not, our support people always confirmed everything with us. No decisions were made without our approval. Usually, I would ask my children for their opinion before reaching our decision, always striving to take into account the feelings of my children, too. Although certain gestures might feel right to me, if the children weren't comfortable with them, I would reject the offer. I had enough trouble understanding my emotions; second-guessing my children was something I had learned to avoid.

Emma, Ian, Matthew, and I were happy to ignore most immediate responsibilities, such as answering the phone or cooking meals. But one thing I felt very strongly about controlling was David's memorial service. As his wife and the mother of his children, I felt obligated to be the one in charge of saying good-bye. I really wanted the children to witness a true testimonial to their father's life, paying a beautiful tribute to a wonderfully deserving man, and I wanted to show the kids my strength by orchestrating it. My behavior those first few days after David's death was vitally important to my children's immediate stability. They were looking to me for guidance and they had to see that I could cope, and that I was still their mother. But the organizing of a funeral or memorial service so quickly after the loss of a loved one is overwhelming and it took a great deal of energy and focus for me. Since the memorial service was eleven days after his disappearance and presumed death, I had the luxury of some time, time to think and plan accordingly.

My family called my church and asked the minister to meet with me. After discussing the format, I set myself a schedule: one day for writing the service and one day for writing my good-bye. I also asked the children to think about working on their contributions. At other moments during different days, I would delegate. But I knew that emotionally I could do only so much in a day because I still had the children to worry about and to tend to. Since it wasn't a funeral, I didn't have the additional stress of speaking with a funeral home.

Although difficult, I stuck with my goal, although the kids didn't want to have anything to do with it and kept putting off what they had agreed to do. I gently reminded them, particularly Emma, about what they had offered to do to help, and I organized and delegated the duties of contacting ushers and readers, as well as asking one friend to buy guest books and pens. The church was kind enough to organize the flowers and reception. I sorted through photographs, as I wanted a collage of David to greet all the guests. I asked my children if they would like to help me sort through the photographs, but they declined. I think that it was too emotional for them. Occasionally, however, one would come into the room and share a few moments glancing at a picture, and I'd try to smile and recall the memory with them. It wasn't until the final deadline that my daughter worked on her written good-bye and designed the cover to the memorial pamphlet.

Up until that point I wasn't sure that she was up to the task and I repeatedly told her that she didn't have to do anything if she didn't feel up to it. But she insisted and persevered, perhaps feeling as I did, that she wanted to do this for her father as a final display of love.

Because people wanted to show their support for the children and me and because David had been so involved in the community and had died in such a public and traumatic way, I knew that many people would attend his service. Because the church holds only about three hundred, I was worried that there wouldn't be enough space. The connecting parish hall also holds upward of three hundred people, so I thought perhaps we could seat people there as well. With complete cooperation and assistance from my minister, speakers, folding chairs, and a video camera were placed in the parish hall so guests could see and hear the service while seated there. The children and I had to then think about who would sit where, and we directed the ushers where to guide certain people.

When the day arrived, about seven hundred people came out to celebrate David's life. It was a wonderful testimony to his forty-seven years. I never considered not bringing my children to the service. Even knowing how emotional and overwhelming the experience would be for them, I knew they had to be there and would come to regret it if they didn't attend. Emma, Ian, and Matthew never said that they didn't want to come, nor did they voice reservations about the event. Growing up, my parents, thinking they were protecting me, never allowed me to go to funerals or memorial services. I vividly remember my first service when my grandmother died. I was twenty-seven years old and I was terrified to be walking into such an overwhelming unknown.

I think it is important for children to go to services for the deceased. It can give them a sense of closure as well as a better understanding of life and death. It gives them a chance to say good-bye. As far as other types of involvement in a service are concerned, such as giving a reading, making a collage, or writing a memory, that involvement can be determined between the child and his or her parent. A child's age, personality, and relationship to the deceased would all play a part in your decision.

Walking into David's service with so many eyes upon us was very difficult, and I give my children a lot of credit. It was a powerful display of support from our community, family, and friends, and my children and I were very touched. Emma, Ian, and Matthew were amazingly strong. They cried as they needed to, but they behaved beautifully. They honored their father well. After the service ended, I stayed until I had greeted and thanked every guest, but my children were exhausted and had had enough, so my brothers and sisters offered to get them out of there and take them home.

One of the hardest aspects of David's death was the publicity of it. If David had died a natural death, I doubt as many as seven hundred people would have turned out for his memorial service. More attention and thus more support were due to the dramatic way in which he was killed. The children and I felt like fish in a very small bowl. The display of caring and concern was comforting yet claustrophobic at the same time. None of us felt as if privacy existed. It is important for friends and family of the bereaved to allow privacy and space to the family. Quiet, undisturbed moments are important for reflection and composure.

Additionally, one-on-one time is essential for a caregiver to devote to a child's needs. My children didn't like being different. With the constant attention and chaos after their father's death, it was hard for them not to feel different. They needed time alone with me. Time to act like a regular family again. Time to cuddle and cry. Time to smile and enjoy one another's company. Time to be just us.

A support person can help a caregiver to identify a family's needs, alerting family and friends to those wishes. Being quite a proud and private family, the children and I had a difficult time accepting everyone's gestures of kindness. Often, people would call or stop by offering to run an errand or cook a meal. Not wanting to inconvenience anyone, we would reject the assistance. It wasn't that we didn't want the help. It was just that we were uncomfortable accepting help and we didn't want to be a burden. It was very awkward.

It took quite some time before we were able to come to terms with people's constant offers of help. Constant willingness wears down the walls of resistance. I eventually realized that just as the children and I needed certain things in grief, my friends and family needed ways to help themselves as well. It wasn't just my immediate family who was grieving. The community, our extended family, and our friends were grieving, too. They needed to help themselves heal by helping us to heal.

If one does want to aid a grieving family, remember to do it from your heart without any expectations. Don't wait for someone to answer the doorbell, call, or write you a note of thanks. Help because you want to. Don't do it for recognition or praise. A bereaved family has enough to focus on. Don't ask them to focus on you as well. A genuine, small gesture such as a caring physical touch or a brief note can mean more than a lavish feast with strings attached. Try not to put pressure on a family suffering from loss with requests or demands.

My children and I were very fortunate to receive as much sincere support as we did. Because of the circumstances, our community reached out to us and aided us in ways that are inconceivable to most individuals. Because we received such amazing support, my children and I were able to focus on our grief, and then on our desire to heal.

One town-wide event organized for my children's benefit was particularly kind. A number of people were concerned about the future education of my children and that of another family in town whose mother had been killed in the same attack. After speaking with some of my close friends, they approached me about a fundraiser. They said that they wanted to have a "great duck race" with the proceeds placed into a trust for my children and the children of the other family.

Friends had volunteered their property and their small stream as the racecourse. Families interested in participating in the race could purchase a rubber duck to enter. Other families wishing to attend the event without racing could buy an entrance ticket at a lesser fee.

The event was planned to take place within ten days. Posters were designed. Food was organized. Activity tables for the children were thought out. Raffle gifts were secured, and even music, cotton candy, and popcorn were not forgotten. Everything seemed set to go, but one major hurdle had yet to be addressed. There was no water in the stream. How were the ducks going to float down toward victory? In an amazing act of community spirit, our town's fire department agreed to run hundreds of gallons of water through the stream on the afternoon of the event. And then it placed firefighters with nets and rods at critical turns in the stream to break up the congestion of massing ducks in the tight turns.

The day of the duck race was warm, sunny, and beautiful. Many of my family were with the children and me for support. The town wasn't sure if we would attend as the race came quite close on the heels of David's death. Except for the memorial service, none of us had been in a large public gathering, and we were terrified of facing a large mass of staring eyes again, but I felt strongly that it was our duty to our town to go and to show our thanks and appreciation. I spoke with my children about it to make sure they were comfortable attending, informing them of my feelings of responsibility. I told them that although no one expected us to attend, I thought it would be nice for us to go. Everyone wanted to see us and to show us how much they cared. The children agreed.

It helped that Emma, Ian, and Matthew had each been given a complimentary duck to race. With their ducks named and ready to go, my children were looking forward to the day.

With the town mayor decked out in costume, sitting in the official judge's chair over the finish line, the preliminary races began. More than 850 people supported or attended the duck race. Since the publicity had been limited to only our town of about 4,000 residents, the turnout was staggering. Although uncomfortable and nervous at first, the children and I managed to try to have fun, though my kids did better than I did. It was wonderful for me to watch my children's smiles and other children's joy.

The families were kind enough to give us some space and to respect how emotional this overwhelming show of support was for us, although my children seemed unfazed, running around chatting with their friends and keeping track of the competition. It was really good for my kids to feel "normal" again, as they downed soda after soda followed by hot dogs and popcorn, not worrying about the stares and comments, just having fun, chasing their ducks down the stream with their friends, finding humor in the giant costumed duck waddling around greeting guests, and, at times, ignoring why we were there.

After the event, although exhausted, I felt wonderful. I envisioned coming away from the day feeling weakened. Instead, I felt a huge surge of strength and renewal. This incredible display of community spirit and support enabled me to move forward. Just when I felt as if I had no more strength to give, a burst of energy was given to me through my community. I couldn't believe how good it made me feel.

As a single parent trying to cope with grieving children, there are times when I really need support. To see that people cared so much about the well-being of my children really comforted me. The knowledge that, should I stumble, someone would always be there for my kids allowed me a deep breath.

The children and I are so very fortunate to be blessed with such a caring and giving community. This show of support was truly unique and wonderful. Not all children suffering grief will be as fortunate as mine. Not all families and friends of the bereaved have the means to organize and produce such a tremendous display of support. And not all grieving families would welcome such a show of support.

As someone concerned about helping a grieving child or family, remember that even a small display of support, any gesture that demonstrates your willingness to help, is important. Love and caring always heal. Simply, respect the personalities of the grieving family and adapt accordingly.

Emotional Support

 THE YEARNING, SADNESS, ANGER, AND LONELI-
ness bred by grief are all emotions that one
has to work through. Emotional support from
family and friends can help a child begin to resolve these
feelings.

Knowing what to say to someone who has lost a loved
one is extremely difficult. Evasion is an easy route but not
always the most helpful. Carefully and sensitively address-
ing the source of grief is usually a better idea. When a child
and parent are involved, there are certain issues to consider.

A misconception that many of my friends and family
had was that David shouldn't be mentioned in front of my
children. Many people were worried that by discussing
David and their various memories of him, Emma, Ian, and

Matthew would get upset. But children operate so very differently from adults. Minutes, hours, days, and/or weeks after hearing about the loss of a loved one, children can frolic, laugh, and behave as if nothing had happened. When others witness this behavior, they assume that the child is fine. They think that this child is coping with his or her grief. An outsider worries that by bringing up the name of a departed loved one, a child will become upset.

I told my family and friends to please mention David around the children. They agreed that they would, but weren't sure how to do it. I explained to them that just as I took my cues from my children when battling grief, so, too, should they. By this I mean you should speak and listen to a child. Don't force the issue, but when you have the attention of a child, speak up, really listen to the child's answers, and take time to reflect on the comments. Ask the child if he misses his dad; or ask her if she feels sad. Don't ask them point blank how they are because you may get an automatic response similar to Matthew's; he always said that he was "fine." Children need a little more direction. Recalling a memory or telling a funny story about a loved one can be a nice thing to do, and it will usually get a child talking, if not thinking, of his or her own memories. When someone has died, the minds of the bereaved are continually focused on the deceased. Few moments go by that are free from thoughts about the departed. As an adult, I wanted to talk about David continually. Emma, Ian, and Matthew couldn't do that, but they could sometimes listen, and I could tell they were often thinking.

Encourage people who feel close to a child to speak up, but remember to know when to be silent. If a loved one is mentioned to a child and the child doesn't say anything, don't press that child for a response. Watch the child and be sensitive to his or her reactions. Children have a hard time voicing their feelings. Instead of talking, children may run away, laugh, or become angry. If a child demonstrates an unusual behavior such as laughing when you are trying to communicate, don't assume that the child is mocking you or taking what you have to say as lighthearted. Both of my boys have a tendency to laugh at very emotional times. Even at their father's memorial service, they would laugh when they weren't crying. Children have a hard time dealing with such powerful emotions. Laughing in times of stress can be an easier escape for them.

So be understanding and patient with a child. Even if a child doesn't respond when a loved one is mentioned, it's all right. Most times a child will probably brush off any comments, but if you don't press too much and are respectful and sensitive to his or her reactions, in time, a child may reach out. They will learn to trust you. Children need opportunities to talk about their loved one. You can support them by gently opening doors to memories and conversation.

As a mother, I encouraged others to initiate conversation with my children. I wanted my kids to be able to talk with someone other than their parent. Perhaps there was something on their minds that they needed to talk about but that they thought would upset me. Maybe they were mad at me and needed to vent their anger to other ears so as to not feel guilty or hurt my feelings.

I also asked parents of my children's peers to talk with their children. I was hoping that my children's friends would feel comfortable talking with them about their dad. Peers are far less threatening to children than adults.

In the end, Ian and Matthew never really found another adult or friend to use as a confidant, and ultimately relied upon me, perhaps because of their personalities or the fact that they were twins and knew that they had each other. But Emma ended up turning to a teacher at her school, with whom she started having daily conversations after classes. One day I approached the teacher, asking her if she ever mentioned Emma's dad. Her reply was no. I suggested that perhaps it would be a good idea since this teacher had also lost her father, and that common understanding and empathy could help Emma to heal. It might benefit both of them.

The teacher agreed to talk with Emma about her father. I was never apprised of any of their conversations but I didn't expect or hope to be. It was between Emma and her teacher and I trusted both of them.

Even now, Emma still talks with her teacher. I am so thankful she has that outlet for her thoughts and feelings. They have a unique bond that, although I can never fully appreciate, reduces my worries. Emma has somewhere to vent and the support from another adult is wonderful.

Other forms of emotional support have been given to my children, support that is less confrontational and more pleasurable for all involved. Frequently, one or more of my brothers or male friends has volunteered to spend time with my children. A male teacher of Ian and Matthew even stepped forward to offer his free time to take the boys on a long hike and then out to lunch. Emma and my sons have been taken by other adults to go skiing, shopping, and golfing, and been treated to professional sporting events, amusement rides, restaurants, and shows. It has proven not only to be a welcome break for me, but when the adult has been a man, it has allowed the children to spend some important alone time with a father figure, which has returned some male influence to their lives.

Guardians of grieving children also need emotional support. In most instances, if a child is grieving, the caregiver is grieving as well, whether it's over the loss of a spouse, a parent, another child, or some other individual who was hugely important in the lives of that particular family. But even if there are occasions when the parent does not grieve, that person will still require some support. Tending to a grieving child is very demanding and exhausting. It allows little time for self-absorption.

There are numerous things that a friend or family member can do to support a caregiver, beginning with simply being a very good listener. Don't bombard the adult with nervous or idle chatter. Silence is better than that. Just spend time with the person and let the individual unload his or her own worries and thoughts. After David died, I really didn't want to talk about anything but David and how his death was affecting our lives. I had no interest in how so-and-so was or where someone went for vacation. I was consumed with thoughts relevant only to our own circle of life. Even indirect topics such as the inquiries surrounding David's death held little interest for me.

Try not to compare or undermine tragedies, either. Hearing the positives after loss isn't appreciated. After the death of a child, to tell a grieving parent that he or she still has another healthy child is not supportive. The parent has still lost a child. No matter how fortunate one's life is beyond a loss, the pain and the hardship of that loss cannot be denied. Acknowledge the weight of that grief and let a person grieve.

Words said to a child or a guardian must be chosen carefully. Just as one should not impose oneself upon a grieving family without an invitation, words, too, should not be uttered without warrant. I vividly remember someone speaking to me once. I had not invited the conversation, but I didn't have the strength to fight it. Suddenly, she was telling me I was a widow. Upon hearing that word "widow," I almost fainted. I hadn't yet processed the thought that I was a "widow." I knew that David was missing, but "widow" hadn't entered my realm of reality yet. For many reasons, it was a very powerful word to hear, and at the age of thirty-nine and given my circumstances, it was very upsetting. Given a different scenario or discussing it with a close family member or friend, I might have had no problem being told that. But from a casual acquaintance standing in my driveway, it stung. Also, keep in mind that there are grieving children in the house or on the property. Although you may think that you are speaking softly, a child has excellent hearing and can pick up more than you might assume. Be very careful with your words.

So be sensitive to the complete picture of grief. Many people are only trying their best to help, but while trying to help, instead of assuming what a family needs to hear or do, take guidance from the bereaved and the situation. In the beginning, don't place too much on their plate either, such as giving a family suggestions for coping, or asking them when and if they plan on writing thank-you letters for meals delivered. Most things can wait until a family requests guidance or may not need to be addressed at all.

After David died, one reality that overwhelmed me and consumed my thought was that I was now my children's only parent. The responsibility felt crushing. The thought that if I were to die, my children would have no one was very frightening. Because of this fear, I knew that I had to take care of myself, and I had to try to get enough rest, food, and exercise to keep my body healthy. Easier said than done. Sleep escaped me, anxiety erased my appetite, and exhaustion left me with no energy. For the first time in my life I came to understand how people suffering from depression literally didn't have the strength to get out of bed. Every morning was a struggle. But my children depended upon me, and because I was their mom, I wasn't going to let them down. What my children *needed* was for me to be reliable, so I had to be there for them.

Thus, I carried on. I ate whenever I could. I slept whenever the time and my body invited it, and I exercised. Before my husband's death, I had been working out at a gym on a fairly regular basis. However, the last thing I was ready to do was throw myself back into that routine. I didn't have the strength and I didn't want to be surrounded by people. I needed to exercise quietly and gently. So, I began yoga. I had tried yoga before and I enjoyed it. After searching television stations, I found a network that had half an hour of yoga every morning. It was great. Not only did it help me to gain my strength back but it also gave me time to clear my mind and to reduce my stress. It helped me to better cope with the needs of my children. I worked the yoga into my daily routine while the children were at school. I refused interruption while working out and ignored my phone. Because I was always worried that the children might be calling me from school, I would always check my messages during the commercials. But aside from that I stayed focused. Sometimes, when my children were home, one or more of them would participate with me in the class. It was fun sharing the experience with them and they seemed to get as much enjoyment out of it as I did.

As a friend or family member, you can encourage some sort of exercise or other stress reducers to help a parent or child combat fatigue and stay healthy. A very young child most likely gets enough exercise exploring his or her world, but even a slightly older child may want to experience the idea of moving to music or bending his or her body in new and unusual ways. The discipline of exercise benefits both the mind and the body, so buy or rent an exercise or yoga video and offer to do the activity with the child or adult to get him or her started. Since I was already used to working out on my own, I chose to do my yoga alone most of the time and I enjoyed the solitariness. But occasionally I preferred the distraction and companionship of friends. If you know the child or adult well, you will figure out what guidance he or she needs.

Before I began my yoga routine, walks were a preferred form of exercise. The distance was not always far, but it was great to get outside. Normally, I wanted to walk somewhere that I wouldn't see anybody I knew. The last thing that I wanted to do on a walk was to be stopped by people expressing their sympathies. Again, I was fortunate enough to have a segment of time to tend to my needs while my children were in school. If you know a parent with a younger child who is grieving, perhaps offering to babysit in order to allow the parent to get away for a while would be a kind gesture. If you have a very young child, walking with your child in a stroller and the company of a friend would benefit both the adult and the child. I liked walking because it gave me pockets of freedom from my house, my children, my phone, my deliveries, and my paperwork. I needed to regroup so that I could stay a positive and supportive mom. I rarely wanted to walk alone. A friend would come over and pick me up and we would drive somewhere. Normally a trail through the woods was nice, as the beauty and tranquillity of nature was soothing for me. We would walk in conversation or in silence, however my mood took me. Before my kids had returned to school, other friends would stay with my children or offer to have them over.

My children also needed to get out of the house and experience a little freedom from their mother. My daughter, Emma, was more often out than she was in. Grieving children need distraction as well. They need time to put aside all the anxiety percolating under their roof. They need to alleviate their stress. A game of tag at a friend's house or a basketball game at a neighbor's is a great offer. As someone wanting to help a grieving family, don't feel that you must offer a tremendous amount of time. Taking children for a bike ride, a game of mini golf, or bowling are some wonderful brief outings that will get them away for a while and afford them a little exercise. While the children are away, the caregiver will have that much-needed time to him- or herself, when he or she can enjoy some peace and rest.

Emotional support can be physical support. By helping a grieving body you are helping a grieving mind. Action leads to healing. Inaction leads to depression. Take your guidance from the grieving family. Don't force them to do something that they are not ready to conquer or that is completely at odds with their lifestyle, but encourage them to build physical strength. Get a tape, take them to an exercise class, take a hike, play tennis, go swimming, dig in the garden with them, or walk with them around a mall. Do whatever they enjoy. Likewise, get their children out. Take them biking, swimming, golfing, running, walking, or strolling around the stores.

Although it does not fall into the category of physical activities, going to the movies, a professional sporting event, or some other form of entertainment is another wonderful outlet and escape. Even just inviting a family over to your house for a few hours to watch a video or for a simple meal is a welcome change. Don't get discouraged or feel rejected, either, if you offer to do something and you are turned down. Offer again at another time. Just because a family says no doesn't mean they don't enjoy your company or suggestion. Certain days bring certain moods, but on a different day, the same suggestion may sound perfect. Don't give up if you really want to help. Just remember to be sensitive with your offers and to give the family space in between your invitations. My children and I would turn down offers but sometimes suggest better times to take up that offer. Grieving families will often give you the lead.

Though this may sound surprising, massages, pedicures, or manicures are wonderful gifts to give a grieving child or adult. They are great stress reducers, and letting someone else pamper you, however briefly, can have a healing effect. Massage, in particular, can be very beneficial. A few months after David died, I decided to cash in on a gift certificate I had received for a massage at my health club, with a massage therapist with whom I was friendly. She knew my situation and would be sensitive to my needs. Rumor had it that she was also very good, so I booked a session. The massage was for one hour, but unbeknownst to me, the therapist spent close to two hours working on unwinding my tightly wound body. The extra time and attention was her subtle gift to me.

I never anticipated how much the massage would affect me. Although my defenses were strongly in place initially, the therapist's expertise soon lowered my guard. Suddenly, I was vulnerable and my emotions began to bubble up. I was determined not to break down and cry during the massage. I wanted to enjoy it and to keep my breathing steady and controlled. But after the session ended, I lost it. I cried hysterically while putting on my robe and washing off the oils in the shower. I couldn't believe how emotional the massage had made me become. I was like a volcano suddenly erupting its core. I was so tired of my tears, and I thought I had some control over them. Grief does things like that. It surprises us. It erupts when we think it is buried.

Of course, one thing that hadn't crossed my mind was that no one had really touched me since David's death. The combination of releasing my stress through intimate physical contact was incredibly powerful. It was very therapeutic but very difficult. It helped me to purge and it was very cathartic, but like all healing in grief, it came at an emotional price.

I continue to get massages every couple of months now. The physical contact is beneficial and the stress release much needed. It becomes less emotional as time goes on, and more pleasurable. Family and friends could combine their resources to make a massage possible. The power of having someone fussing over you and being relaxed and pampered should never be underestimated. As I suggested earlier, even a pedicure or manicure is wonderful. When the time is right, take a grieving mother and daughter out for a pedicure with their friends and make it a fun, social gathering. My daughter loved having her nails done. If weather permits, bring along a picnic and relax in a park afterward. Use your imagination and don't be afraid of letting the laughter flow.

Spiritual support is another important element of emotional support. A family's religious beliefs can help to sustain them through the painful time of grief. Offering to drive them to religious services or offering to purchase books on spirituality might be a valuable assistance.

When someone close to you dies, there are so many unanswerable questions. Is that person all right? Will I ever sense their presence? Will I see them again? Can they hear and see me now? All three of my children had these same thoughts. Some wondered more often than others. Matthew was continually trying to grasp the uncertainty of death. When I would go in to say good night to him, he would start questioning me about the universe and its dimensions. He never specifically mentioned his father when we discussed these topics, but clearly, the concerns for his father had instigated his thought process. I attempted to answer Matthew as best I could. Occasionally I would turn the conversation around to David or the question of life after death, encouraging Matthew to believe that his father was at peace and in another spiritual realm watching over him.

Life after death is a tricky discussion to have with children after the loss of a loved one. I wanted all my children to believe that David was at peace and watching over us as our guardian angel. I also wanted them to think that he was content, even happy, in his new environment. I told my children that of course their dad missed being with us, but he was okay and in no pain. He was still with us, only in a different way now. The difficult part of this discussion was that I didn't want to paint too rosy a picture of the afterlife, but I needed to talk about it because I wanted my children to feel secure in their father's place in the universe. After the death of a loved one, it is very difficult to know exactly what goes on in the mind of a child. I was worried that if I idealized death and the afterlife, my children might want to join their father. I didn't want any of them contemplating suicide. So I had to carefully choose my words to comfort but also to make them aware of the problems of death. I told them that although one is at peace after one dies, life is precious and wonderful and being able to touch and hug each other should be relished. Eating an ice cream cone or going to the beach are earthly pleasures we should enjoy while we are able. Their daddy was now in heaven to watch over them. He would want them to live and to enjoy life until it was their time to join him, hopefully at a very old age. Their father would want them to go on living.

My children needed to hear me give them these reassurances. Other children from different families with different backgrounds may not need the same support. Ian, however, had concerns. Although he desperately wanted his father to be all right, he was terrified of his dad's spirit visiting him. Matthew voiced a few worries about the same issue but seemed to come to terms with it rather quickly. Ian, on the other hand, didn't. It was fine with him, even welcoming, for David's spirit to visit a sibling or myself, but he wanted no part of it. I reassured him that his father would understand his wishes. Daddy would know that Ian didn't want a visit during the night and he would stay out of his room. Besides, I told him, the chances of David visiting any of us would be pretty slim, as seeing spirits is not a normal occurrence. I don't know many people who'll admit to it even if they have. One's never quite sure if it's a dream.

My long chats with Ian seemed to help him. But I wonder if perhaps that was one of the reasons he chose to sleep with his light on for so long after his father's death. Although he has little trouble sleeping now and never keeps his light on, he is still terrified of a chance visit.

Even with Ian's fears of ghosts, I still believe that my discussions with my children about life after death were warranted. Ian's worries could have still been there had I not mentioned anything. Cartoons, videos, and books often address the possibility of ghosts. By not discussing the issue, I don't believe I would have shielded him from his fear. At least I provided him with a platform for voicing his anxiety.

The uncertainties of death and afterlife are frightening. As a parent I had to console my children. I had to give them security, even if I had my own doubts. I had just as many questions as my children. Although I appeared confident to them, I had my own need for security, and I was honest with them about my inability to answer some of their questions. They knew that I didn't have all the answers, and they just had to trust that their dad was okay. They had to have faith.

I am not a deeply religious person, but I am very spiritual. I believe in the afterlife and spirits, and I believe in another dimension to this universe. Still, I was searching for confirmation, and I wanted someone else to tell me David was all right.

Many events occurred just before and after David died

that helped me. I remember the night before David died; I was sitting in front of the television flicking through channels when I came upon a psychic named Jonathan Edwards. Choosing to keep my deep spirituality private, I had never reached out to psychics before, and I had never heard of Mr. Edwards. But I became engrossed in his ability and found it comforting and intriguing. That evening after David and I had gone to bed, I began to discuss the show with him and the concept of life after death. After talking for a while and recounting some of the examples from the show, I asked David about his beliefs. There he was, with his light on, sitting up in bed, appearing to be attentive, but fast asleep. I guess I got my answer. It made me laugh.

The next day, David was killed. I lay in bed that night crying and trying to find comfort. I recalled the show from the night before and wondered if it was really the truth. Was David in a better place and at peace? Was he aware of our pain and would I ever feel his presence? At some point during the long night as I lay in my bed unable to find sleep and becoming more and more anxious, I felt something. I wasn't searching for it; it just came as I was trying to calm myself down with deep breathing. His presence. As I lay on my stomach, I could feel David's body lying on top of mine, arm over arm, leg over leg, and torso over torso. It was as if he was using the weight of his body to comfort me and to let me know that everything was all right. It wasn't frightening but rather wonderful. I had absolutely no doubt that he was with me and doing what he could to calm me. There were no words or visions, just a sense of presence. It was very powerful. Many people in my support group had similar experiences, albeit in differing ways. It was as if their loved one was reaching out to them to let them know they were all right. It was amazing.

After I knew that David had perished and my children had accepted his death, I told my children about what had happened to me that first night. I told them that I had sensed their father had come to let us know that he was okay. I didn't elaborate or bring it up repeatedly. I just thought that perhaps they would find comfort in it as I did. They just listened and didn't question my experience, but rather, they seemed to acknowledge understanding and indeed some comfort.

Even though I felt certain of my beliefs, I still had questions. I wanted someone to tell me with absolute certainty that David was fine. Of course, I knew that that was impossible, but I was going to search until I had come to terms with his death. I needed that spiritual support to help me give my children the strength they required in order to heal. Religious leaders are a wonderful source of confirmation for grieving families. Other people may choose less conventional methods or a combination of ways. I spoke with my minister but I also wanted something else, and many people in my support group had discussed going to see a psychic. Some had already gone. I was hesitant to visit a psychic, as not all psychics may be legitimate. Indeed some people don't believe in them at all, but I was curious.

Then one day, a friend of mine, not knowing my thoughts, suggested that she take me to see a psychic who had helped her before. I was nervous because I certainly didn't want to hear anything traumatic, but I desperately needed reassurance as to David's situation. So I went.

My friend took me and drove me home. It was an extremely emotional experience and not something that I would recommend for everyone, particularly not young or impressionable children. But I came away comforted, even if the comfort was falsely placed. I knew everything said wasn't reality, but that was okay. It enabled me to hold on to hope, to believe my intuition, and to trust my beliefs. It helped me to voice some of my worries that I might have otherwise withheld. For me, there was catharsis as well as a knowledge that this wasn't something that I would need to do again. My curiosity had been calmed.

As a friend or family member, be careful when guiding a child or adult down this path of spiritual support. A trained professional or religious leader is a certain and safe avenue, and they should always be the first attempt for comfort. But if a grieving child or adult is searching for a less conventional spiritual support, be cautious for them. A grieving individual is vulnerable, and being taken advantage of or put through unnecessary emotional pain could cause additional trauma. Make sure that the individual is up for the reality of a psychic and make sure to escort that person and stay there in the event that the person needs to leave. But don't walk away if the grieving person really feels that he or she needs to go. Rather than rushing into it, just be there for that individual and encourage him or her to take plenty of time and to think about the idea. In grief, haste is never a good idea. Questions may become answered and beliefs secured over time, so burning desires on one day may vanish the next. Encourage a family in grief to take deep breaths and to think, as sometimes reason is needed. The children and I needed our heads sometimes more than our hearts to combat the grieving process. Logic and desire must work together.

Creative outlets are good ways for children to deal with their grief. Since children can often have trouble voicing their worries and thoughts, creativity is a good way for un-leashing them. Different children may want different outlets. While some children may want to draw pictures, others might want to build something or play with dolls. You could buy a child some crayons and paper, clay, age-appropriate woodworking supplies, or felt pieces and glue. You could take a child to an art store and let him or her pick out what's interesting. Enrolling a child in an art class or taking a child to an art exhibit are other possibilities. Photography, creative writing, or drama classes can be good options for older children.

Music and writing became a wonderful outlet for my children and me. The creative process of writing gave Emma and me strength, and music brightened us all up as well as alleviating some of our stress. In the evenings, when we were alone, the children and I would dance. We started doing this because one night, we put on a CD that one of the children had given David. We danced to the music that he enjoyed and smiled. Later on, I went out and bought a radio to put in our kitchen. Many evenings we would crank up the music and boogie down, releasing our inhibitions and cares. It was great for all of us and it gave us a new bonding experience.

Go out and buy some music for a grieving family. Get something that you think they would like given their tastes. Don't worry if the music is silly or insignificant. The family can always save it for when they feel up to it. If there is a movie that you know they enjoyed, go out and purchase the soundtrack for it. For very young children, a silly or light-hearted soundtrack may be just what they need. To see a child laugh soon after loss is wonderful for both the child and the adult.

Here are other creative ideas for those wishing to help: Invite a child over for a play date and help him or her make a video on a camcorder with friends. Involve grieving children in acting classes or playwriting or take them to see a play or musical. You could send them a diary, scrapbook, or poetry books, or help them to design, build, and maintain a small garden. Encourage a child to use creative outlets without being pushy and come to understand a family's needs during grief so you can provide the resources to fill those needs.

A grieving family needs time and space; don't expect an immediate answer to a question or thanks for your kindness. If you want to send a card or place a phone call, make sure to tell a family that a response is not necessary. I received hundreds of sympathy cards and phone calls, and there was no possible way that I could respond to every one. The thought of doing so totally stressed me out. As a friend, be sensitive to that. A gesture of kindness should be done because you want to, not because you expect something in return.

When making a phone call or writing a note, many people have no idea what to say. Multiple cards and messages began with "I don't know what to say." When I was in their position, as someone offering condolences, I never knew what to say, either. But don't let that hold you back from reaching out. Acknowledgments of sympathy with uncertain thoughts are much better than no acknowledgment at all. It is disappointing when a good friend is too unsure or afraid to reach out. A simple "I'm so sorry" or "We will miss your father very much" was all that we needed. No one expects anyone to have all the answers. Say what is in your heart and be sincere, and if you can't do that, then a silent hug or touch of the arm is enough. It takes courage to confront someone who is grieving. But with that strength of courage you are giving strength to the bereaved. You are helping them to heal.

Kindness and support are cyclical. The more that one reaches out to others, the more others will reach out to you in times of need. Simple gestures suffice. Don't ask "What can I do?" Just do it. A grieving family might feel uncomfortable asking for support. Take that burden off the family and demonstrate your support with actions. Letting others know you care is life sustaining.

Practical Support

EMOTIONAL SUPPORT IS VITAL, BUT EVERYDAY practical support is equally important. Many people may find that offering practical support is an easier and less awkward way of helping out a grieving family.

The Simplest of All Gestures: Food

Encouragement, love, and guidance were needs for my children and me, but so was food. It took me many months before I was able to settle back into a routine of preparing family dinners again. Dinnertime had always been an evening ritual in our family, but after my husband's death, the thought of cooking had lost all appeal for me. Breakfast and lunch were easy enough, but dinner was something else. Not only did I not have the energy to cook, I also didn't want to face our altered evening routine. What would I do to our routine now that David and I couldn't have our quiet meal together? How would the children and I fill the time?

I needn't have worried about filling my time. Between the children, the phone, and everything else that had to get done, time was something that I needed more of. As far as our routine, that was solved for us. I ate with my children and our schedule became dependent upon the delivery of our meals, provided by our support network.

Immediately following the news of David's death, we began to receive gifts of food, including multiple meals that would arrive at the same time. We had so much food, we weren't sure what to do with it all. Luckily, much of it could go into the freezer, and after a few days, a friend of mine stepped in to coordinate the delivery.

Somehow, my friend got word out that she was in charge of food, and that anyone wishing to deliver a meal should contact her first. When people called or stopped by offering to bring food, I would tell them to contact my friend to make arrangements, and before long, everything was organized. Every day, my friend would tell me who was bringing us a meal and around what time. The children and I set our dinner schedule around the approximate time of delivery. Occasionally, meals would need to be heated or prepared in some small way. If that were the case, we would normally receive the food well before dinnertime. Of course, there were individuals who didn't know about the food chain and just dropped off meals anyway, and sometimes there was mis-communication and we wouldn't get a meal one day, but get two the next. My freezer filled quickly.

If a friend or family member would like to bring over a meal, I would suggest something that can be frozen. Though we initially received more than enough food, it was comforting to me to know that after the meal deliveries died down, I would still have food in my freezer for the kids.

If a friend can't organize meals, a local church or synagogue may be able to assist. Many houses of worship organize members to deliver food on a daily basis. They are usually well-coordinated and experienced volunteers.

After a short time, when the freezer was stuffed to capacity, it became evident that my children and I were receiving far too much food. As we always had plenty of leftovers, I called my friend coordinating deliveries and asked her to drop off meals only every other day. Eventually, we asked to receive meals only twice a week. Within two to three months, aside from the occasional surprise dinner, we had stopped asking for food altogether. It wasn't that we didn't appreciate it. It was just that our family needed to return to some sort of normalcy and that normalcy included my cooking.

In most cases, food is always a welcome gift. If you can't cook or don't have time, a bag of groceries is also a great idea. As I wasn't up to going to the supermarket, breakfast and lunch supplies were wonderful. Even a carton of milk and a loaf of bread were appreciated. Rather than sending flowers, consider a food basket. We received a lovely basket of croissants, jams, and bagels. Decide what the family might like and do what you can.

When food or meals were delivered, they were often just left by the door or put on my kitchen table. We didn't feel like talking with everyone who stopped by, so people were sensitive to our privacy. When my friend called me each day with an update on the delivery, she would let me know who was delivering the meal and ask me where I wanted the food left. Often the people would come and go without even ringing the doorbell, and many of them I didn't even know.

In addition to a homemade meal or groceries, consider buying something already prepared. My children became very tired of the same type of food, such as pasta, soups, chicken, or meatloaf, so the occasional taco kit or pizza was always a big hit. Find out what type of fast food the children like and take their orders. Although a nice home-cooked meal was enjoyable, the children loved the infrequent milk shake and fries. Simple prepared food is not always something to feel embarrassed about delivering.

Other Types of Practical Support

The list of practical support is enormous, and much of the practical support is directed toward the guardian because the guardian is the one responsible for overseeing the welfare of the children. In order for the guardian to focus on the children's needs, the guardian needs to have some of his or her responsibilities lifted. By alleviating these responsibilities from a parent or guardian, you are indirectly benefiting a child. But as well as indirectly helping a grieving child, with ideas that I will discuss later, there are other things that can be done that more directly benefit a child.

Shortly after the death of their father my boys received from a friend a card along with a video game. My sons love computer games, so they were thrilled, but more lasting was the note accompanying the present, and my sons still remember its message. Written in the hand of a child, it said, "Presents always make me feel better when I'm sad, hopefully they make you feel better too." This simple act of kindness and acknowledgment of grief offered Ian and Matthew both emotional and practical support, and it was very meaningful for them.

Because of the circumstances of David's death, we received a fair amount of cash and checks in the mail, often sent by strangers or anonymously, and most of the time, the notes read "for the children." With the money, I would take Emma, Ian, and Matthew to the movies, treat them to a meal, or allow them a gift. I felt uncomfortable accepting the money but I rationalized it by spending it on the children, and I came to accept the reality that others needed to offer something to my children and me. They needed to come to terms with their own grief that they felt for our family, and by sending us money, it helped them to heal as well.

Although not as exciting as meals out or video games, there are other types of support children will need. Teeth still need to be professionally cleaned, doctors need to be visited, and soccer practices attended, so you could offer to set up dental visits or annual doctor's appointments, as well as offering to drive the children to their various appointments, staying with them if necessary. You may want to organize a carpool and get other families involved to lessen your own burden and to ease the guilt of the parent. If one person is doing all the driving, a parent might be hesitant to call on that individual with concern that he or she is imposing too much. Additionally, you could gather a list of willing chaperones or chauffeurs for the children and tape it to the refrigerator door in the grieving family's home.

Babysitting a child or inviting the child over for a play date can be a big help. If a parent has to visit an attorney, or stand in line at Motor Vehicles or the Department of Social Security, dragging along a child can be torment for both parties. Ease a child's stress by alleviating the emotional trauma and physical boredom of these mundane responsibilities. These tasks are challenging enough without the additional concern of a child.

The list of practical needs goes on and on, and it may take anywhere from a few months to a few years for a grieving family to get all the details resolved. I still have things that I have put off. It's not that I can't do these chores; it's just that I don't want to because I want to spend time enjoying my life with my children instead of pushing paperwork or waiting endlessly on hold on the phone. Below are some ways that you can indirectly help a child by alleviating some of the guardian's responsibilities and thus allowing that person to spend more time with his or her grieving child.

One of the first things that a parent may need to do is find an estate attorney. New wills appointing different beneficiaries or guardians may need to be drawn up, existing wills may need to be filed, and many other legal procedures may need to be addressed as assets may have been left to a child. Living arrangements may also need to be altered. Children will need to be considered in any of these steps, and for that reason, it is extremely important for a parent to find a good attorney.

I knew that I needed an attorney but I had no idea where to begin. Fortunately, my siblings stepped in and helped me. I always feel that the best way to find a good professional is by referrals, and my sister knew some good attorneys in her town, so she contacted them and asked for a referral of someone in my area. My brother also looked into leads from people such as my insurance agent and accountant, and interviews were quickly arranged for when my brother was able to take some time off work to accompany me.

If you are helping someone in need to search for an estate attorney, make sure your friend or relative is comfortable with his or her potential attorney. Personality or attitude on the part of both parties may be the determining factor. The parent or guardian will be spending a great deal of time speaking with this attorney so it is important for that caregiver to feel at ease. Also, offer to be present during the interview process. I wasn't able to concentrate particularly well and I didn't have the energy to take much in the way of notes, so another set of ears helped me with my decision process, and questions that eluded me were addressed by my brother. If a parent insists upon privacy and wants to speak with the attorney alone, encourage your friend or family member to bring along a tape recorder. Although he or she must inform the attorney that the session will be taped, at least the caregiver will have a recording of what transpired, allowing him or her to review any facts or uncertainties, and prompting further questions to ask the attorney in a follow-up interview.

In addition to securing an attorney, finding an accountant may also be important. Unless one has the knowledge, desire, and time to research all the tax implications of death, especially a sudden one, an accountant is helpful. I know that I had no desire to deal with all the financial issues surrounding David's passing, and, frankly, I didn't have the time. So, if you know an accountant who is willing to offer help, suggest his or her services.

A professional financial advisor can be very useful. Personally, I had little involvement with our financial situation as David earned the family income, paid the bills, and managed our portfolio. I knew squat. After he died, aside from my concerns about the children, my second biggest fear was our financial situation. How would I manage? What were our assets and what were our debts? How will I pay for my children's education? And what would I do with any money coming in? I knew nothing about stocks, bonds, or other forms of investments, so I really needed trustworthy guidance.

Again, my support network of friends and family researched referrals and made suggestions. Interviews were set up and my brother took off more time from work to accompany me. Happily, we found a company with whom I felt comfortable.

It is very important when handing over assets to do your research. Even in times of grief, unscrupulous people may be looking to take advantage of a situation. To lose a loved one and then to lose all one's assets would be truly devastating. Bring along an objective and clear-minded friend or family member to help with your judgment. On all of my interviews, I came away with the same opinions and feelings as my brother, and it was reassuring to have that confirmation, as it made me more comfortable with my decisions.

Even if you don't want a financial advisor for continued advice, an initial meeting with an expert in this field would help to point a grieving family in the right direction. Getting together a list of expenses and income and setting up a new budget help to guide a family down the right path. For me, obtaining the knowledge that sound financial decisions were being made in my children's best interest relieved a great deal of stress. When questions arose regarding the children's education, the portfolio, or the home mortgage, there was always a direction for me to turn. It was one less worry, and it was one more protection for the children.

Even if a family has little or no assets, speaking with a financial expert or accountant is advisable. Perhaps there are ways to adjust a budget or find a suitable investment that will help the family's overall financial picture, and although these services require money, the peace of mind and security they provide may be of tremendous value. If you know a trusted friend who works as a professional in any of these fields, he or she may be willing to offer some help, perhaps offering a discount or even waiving his or her fee. However, think carefully about your comfort level of giving such personal details to a friend, and the impact it may have on your friendship. How a family chooses to get financial advice after the death of a loved one is a personal choice, but certainly an estate attorney is a necessity when a parent dies and children, who must be provided for and protected, are involved.

Friends and family members who live far away can help with routine phone calls and paperwork. After a death, families—and especially children who have lost a parent—may be entitled to certain government or insurance benefits. As a friend or family member you could call the Department of Social Security to find out if the grieving family is entitled to any benefits and what the procedure is to apply. Workers' compensation or union benefits may also be awarded. When my friends or family members called various organizations for me, they were sometimes given the information without my involvement. Often forms needed to be sent and filled out, so the initial contact did not necessarily have to be from me. Other times, when someone would contact an organization for me, I would have to be on the phone as well, confirming the information or answering more-specific questions. If the deceased was employed at the time of his or her death, perhaps a friend could call the employer and inquire about any policies to which the family is entitled. As my husband was the sole health insurance carrier, I knew that the children and I needed to speak with David's employer about a COBRA health insurance extension.

The burden of practical needs—including the seemingly endless amounts of paperwork—may often feel paralyzing. Copies of birth certificates, death certificates, and marriage certificates may need to be obtained, and I seemed to be making copies continually. Social Security and reference numbers may need to be easily accessible, so perhaps a close family member could compile a list of such necessary information and phone numbers and place it in a central location, thus saving a grieving family the additional bother of digging through paperwork. Buying and labeling folders for items such as Social Security documents, wills, or sympathy cards and purchasing containers for these folders is another small gesture that will be greatly appreciated.

On the heels of death, getting in touch with the Department of Motor Vehicles about transferring a car's registration appears not only trivial but also inconsequential. Nothing seems to matter except the absence of the loved one and the pain endured by that absence. However, tending to these responsibilities must be done, and this is another area where others can help.

At some point after David's death, I became aware that our car registrations, titles, and loans were in David's name, and this was going to have to be changed, especially since I knew that I would eventually need to sell David's car. The cost of upkeep and insurance on two cars was expensive and, with only one driver in the family, an unnecessary expense. I asked a friend of mine to call Motor Vehicles for me to find out what needed to be done. She also called my car's financing company to find out what they required. Multiple copies of death certificates and other documentation were needed and it was far from simple. After months of miscommunication, it was finally sorted out, but at one point I became so frustrated and distraught that my attorney had to get involved. Unfortunately, on occasion, simple problems become complicated ones.

Once things were sorted out with David's car, I wanted to sell it. It had only been a short while since David's death and my children weren't happy about getting rid of the car. Emma really wanted to hold on to it until she could drive and use it for herself, but she was four years away from that. Truthfully, it was too painful for me to have the car in the driveway staring silently at us, and I didn't like having to continually worry about driving and maintaining it. Every time I would take it out for an errand and then return up our driveway, my children would always fleetingly think and hope it was their father coming home again, and I couldn't continue to torture them or myself with this painful illusion. So, against my children's wishes, my brother-in-law came over to help me find a buyer for the car. While I stayed hidden, he approached dealers asking the value of the car and if they were interested. After a few hours, a deal was struck and David's car was gone. Perhaps had I been more willing to devote more time, I would have gotten a better deal, but I wanted to make the process as quick and simple as possible because it was too painful, and I was anxious to get home to the children.

Now that the car was sold, I needed to return to the Department of Motor Vehicles, turn in the car license plates, and cancel David's license. If a car is sold, the license plates must be returned, and regardless, a license of someone deceased must be turned in. This is very important to do because it will protect you and your children from fraud. If neither item is returned, other individuals can steal the information, causing large debt or other headaches for a grieving family. False identities can be created from stolen information.

On a related note, be very careful about who receives Social Security numbers. Organizations may ask for Social Security numbers for either the parent or the child in order to process information or benefits. Again, identities can be stolen, so you should take great caution when revealing any information, and be especially cautious on the phone. People will and do take advantage of the vulnerable, so always check a source. Don't be afraid to question why certain information is needed, and get a friend to help if you are uncertain. If there is any doubt, don't hand out the information until you feel more comfortable with the situation, and take your time. Many things can be handled another day.

Unfortunately, the list doesn't end there, and now that our car was sold, I had to get in touch with my insurance company. This was not an immediate need since once I produced the sales receipt, my insurance remittance would become effective from that date of sale, so I did have time. But I did want to get it all behind me. Knowing certain bills were smaller was comforting from a financial standpoint.

Even if a family doesn't sell a car, it is a good idea to touch base with your insurance agent. Finances could have changed and life insurance policies may have been awarded. Understanding your policies with regard to homeowners and auto insurance is never a bad idea. I knew nothing about how our policies were structured, and I had no idea when payments were due. I felt that I had a responsibility to my children to understand these things and to structure our policies in a way that was advantageous to our new situation. By discussing various options with my insurance agent, I was able to obtain a better understanding of my coverage and to alter some things.

Life insurance is usually another important issue when it comes to children. If there was no life insurance for the deceased and you, as the remaining parent or guardian, don't have an agent, consider obtaining a policy from a trusted professional. If you do have a policy, perhaps that policy needs to be changed in the aftermath of a death. As a widowed parent, there may be substantial estate taxes owed by your beneficiaries, who are normally your children, upon your death. Life insurance policies can be a good way to offset those taxes, ensuring enough assets will be available to cover the expenses of your death, and that there will be enough money to go to your children in the event that they are left parentless at a young age.

Although this concept is frightening to think about, every eventuality needs to be addressed in regard to children. Speak with your accountant and estate attorney before deciding what is right for your family. There are other avenues to explore. An insurance agent is always happy to sell another policy, so get a clear understanding of the situation before approaching an agent. Give yourself time to think about things and encourage a friend or family member to go along with you on the interview process, and again, don't make any hasty decisions.

With the death of a loved one, financial resources may be significantly, if not altogether, depleted, and if a child is attending college, nursery school, or some other private education, scholarships may need to be looked into. As a friend or family member, you could contact the school for information and suggestions about alternative funding and resources. Likewise, as was the case with our situation, health insurance may need to be investigated. Getting quotes and gathering information is a tremendous project—and investigating all the details is a job that many guardians would be happy to hand over to a trusted friend.

Friends can make many other phone calls for a grieving family. You may need to change the contact person on household bills and credit cards, for example. My brother went through my files for me and wrote a list of credit card companies and utility companies that needed to be contacted regarding David's death. A friend or family member can gather this information, and then make calls, when permitted by the company's procedures, or collect the necessary documentation to be mailed. Stamps can be bought to save a family a trip to the post office.

While this may sound trivial on the heels of a serious discussion of finances and insurance, there are other types of "benefits"—such as frequent flier miles or other types of reward plans—that may need to be transferred. Getting in touch with an airline may be a huge help as this is exactly the kind of detail that is low priority. Perhaps a family wants to get away for a change of scenery, but is worried about the expense. If air miles had been accrued, in the name of the deceased, substantial savings may be available, allowing a family to escape for a short while. Don't be afraid to make these types of suggestions or arrangements. Just helping with hotel reservations can be a nice idea.

Not everything on a "to do" list will get accomplished in a grieving household. Things will need to be prioritized, and many responsibilities will have to be completed by the parent or guardian. Mowing the lawn, collecting leaves, pulling weeds, and shoveling snow might be tasks that are less important but that still need to get done. Don't be afraid to step forward and offer such seemingly "insignificant" assistance.

By helping a grieving family in any way, you are helping a child to heal. If you directly help a child, or indirectly, because you are freeing a guardian of responsibility and enabling that caregiver to focus his or her energies on a grieving child, your emotional or practical support will help a family to guide a child through grief. Routine, love, honesty, security, and emotional and practical support are all what children need when they grieve.

Checklist of Needs:
What a Friend or Family Member Can Do

 BELOW ARE JUST SOME EXAMPLES OF SUGGES-
tions discussed in the previous chapters on how,
when applicable, to help a family, child, or
guardian in grief.

WHAT YOU CAN DO FOR A CHILD

- ❏ Listen.
- ❏ Buy arts and crafts supplies.
- ❏ Take a child out to the movies, a sporting event, a bike ride, or an art exhibit.
- ❏ Initiate a play date for a child.
- ❏ Allow for creative outlets such as gardening, journaling, or dancing.

❑ Give a gift of a manicure, pedicure, or massage.

❑ Focus your attention on a child.

❑ Talk about the lost loved one.

❑ Pick up food from a favorite restaurant.

❑ Investigate exercise options like yoga or hiking.

What You Can Do for a Family

❑ Organize counseling, or locate support groups or children's bereavement camps.

❑ Contact a religious leader.

❑ Contact schools, teachers, and guidance counselors.

❑ Look into scholarship possibilities or other available financial resources.

❑ Organize food delivery or cook a meal.

❑ Offer to chauffeur or chaperone children.

❑ Do yard work.

❑ Do laundry or other household chores.

❑ Send a card.

❑ Set up dental and doctor visits, then provide transportation.

What You Can Do for a Parent or Guardian

❑ Find an estate attorney.

❑ Find an accountant.

❑ Find a financial planner.

❑ Contact the deceased's employer for benefits.

❑ Check health care coverage.

- ❐ Contact Social Security and/or workers' comp.
- ❐ Find a life insurance agent.
- ❐ Check homeowners and auto insurance policies.
- ❐ Find a funeral home.
- ❐ Handle paperwork.
- ❐ Help sell a car.
- ❐ Contact the Department of Motor Vehicles to cancel a license or change registration.
- ❐ Contact credit card companies and other household accounts to change contact information or to cancel.
- ❐ Switch air miles.

Professional Sources of Guidance

LISTED BELOW ARE SOME OF THE MENTAL health resources available nationwide, in Canada, and in some United States commonwealths and territories. Most mental health resources are found locally and a few are organized nationally. Certain states have more resources than others. Looking in the government section of a local phone book under social, human, or family services is one way to begin. Contacting your local religious leader, pediatrician, school guidance counselor, or hospital is perhaps an easier alternative.

Alliance of Information & Referral Systems, www.airs.org or *www.211.org,* or call 211 where available. Referral system currently being developed throughout the United States and Canada. The organization will inform individuals about local resources for mental health needs.

National Mental Health Association, www.nmha.org, 1-800-969-NMHA(6642). A resource for finding information and counseling.

Catholic Charities, www.catholiccharitiesusa.org, 1-703-549-1390. Nonsectarian services for mental health needs. Available in Canada and some U.S. commonwealths and territories. Anyone, regardless of faith, is able to use these services.

Jewish Family Services. Available throughout the United States. Nonsectarian services for mental health needs. No central Web site address or phone number. Call 411 or look in the Yellow Pages for your local agency. Local Web sites can be accessed. Anyone, regardless of faith, is able to use these services.

The Dougy Center for Grieving Children, www.grievingchild.org, 1-503-775-5683. A reference Web site for grieving children and their families.

Comfort Zone Camp, www.comfortzonecamp.org, 1-866-488-5679. A bereavement camp for children.

Index